to go without blinking

poems by Aimee Herman

BlazeVOX [books]
Buffalo, NY

BlazeVOX

Thank you to the following journals/presses where some of these poems appear in (sometimes) a slightly different variation: self-diagnosed lactose intolerance (Baobob Tree Press), *Sous Les Paves,* Oysters & Chocolate, InStereo Press, Soundzine, and/or journal, Spiny Babbler Press, Brooklyn Paramount, Downtown Brooklyn, Pulp, Queerocracy Zine, and Overpass Books.

For those that exist beyond borders, languages, scar tissue, hair growth, childhood, gender, sexuality, thread count, word count, degrees, titles, posture, blood, genetics, diagnoses, hate, love, time.

[A specific thank you and heavy burst of gratitude to j/j/ hastain, Quetzo J. Herejk, and my dad]

"Pain is ugly, but survival isn't"   --Daphne Gottlieb

Table of Contents

to go without blinking

prologue:

leave a trace, leave a smell

elastic minus the girdle

There is no need for synthetics like Victoria's whispered, overpriced secret. Allow space for binding, packing, a push down or spackle.

to write to fill   the
lines where splinters
                exhale
            off benches

This body of text practices trilingualism and contraction. Theories include gender confiscation and syntax dissection. Calls herself alone with pen ink plastic cap between lips, kissing language of stain and blots. There is no need for love when paper exists and never interrupts or walks away.

to remove the veins attached to initials
orientations

There may be a carve out. A distinction between childhood trauma and mother carnage.

need to declare a bra size
sharp accent to disconnect
                    the unwanted

I know I have long hair but sometimes I am boy. When I talk about my dick I need you to believe that I have one [sometimes].

write in scars and exit signs
stain of conformity and academic line structure

There is no need for paper distinctions, map assurances, stick-on-peel-off labels. The location of this text-body may be found in Whitman songs and Bukowski contradictions. Reveal the gesticulation of body's remorse: call it dirty piece of nothingness or ghostly or passed around or workshopped. How can one edit the typos found in scar tissue. Poem.

bruises like brooklyn sidewalks
the stick stickiness   stitches   stitching

Scars are a language learned only by breathing.

confuse memory with medicine
scream down spine.   paper cuts.   signature
steam
          permanence.

this poem is queer with white disco blood cells, turning over floor boards purchased from mice and roaches with a lineage of two hundred million years ago

do not lock lips with this poem because your bed sore against this lip sore could lead to the need for medication in the form of cream or humiliation and I am quite sure your health insurance, if you even have any, will not begin to cover the cost of it

this poem has been diagnosed with HPV, gonorrhea, syphilis, ADD, chlamydia, dyslexia, candidiasis, scabies, malaria, herpes, high blood pressure, cataracts, genital warts, PTSD, lactose intolerance, and bacterial vaginosis

this poem votes Republican, but calls itself a Democrat or does not vote at all due to overactive sleep cycle, laziness and the inability to pick a side

this poem needs to hire an accountant to keep track of its sexual partners

this poem steals prescriptions from medicine cabinets and bedside tables

this poem is into coarse language, orgies, erections, blow jobs, humiliation and the word **NO**

this poem places pills in pockets for later when it is hungry and too tired to steam up broccoli or cocaine

this poem hates white people and yuppies and those with 401K's and retirement plans and women with quick metabolisms and personal trainers and anyone who contributes to over-population

this poem has a bomb attached to its belly, distended from starvation because it chose an eating disorder over trichotillomania because emaciation is more socially acceptable than baldness

this poem fingers itself on a Monday in the bathroom of over-priced university and foregoes hand washing in order to wipe poem juice on door knobs and hand shakes

this poem picks its nose and initiates a storm of blood rising from cartilage toward cleft above lip

this poem has a weakened immune system due to nutritional laziness and inaccessible health insurance this poem does not know how to handle guns, a tube of lipstick, heavy machinery, and men

this poem straddles guns, organic carrots, umbrella handles, chicken sausage, harmonicas, drum sticks, thermoses, and does not wash after use

this poem packs an elastomer cock purchased for twenty-five dollars plus tax minus 10% for being the floor model

this poem has stolen chapstick, salad dressing, a karaoke machine, several glasses of beer from men expecting conversation or drunk touching, two cream cheese sesame bagels, a cup of coffee

this poem will fuck you for currency as long as she can send in her understudy to complete the transaction

this poem ran out of lubricant and found feces to be a fine alternative

this poem needs to tell someone about the time her ~~uncle~~ ~~babysitter~~ ~~dentist~~ ~~music teacher~~ ~~neighbor~~ ~~ex-boyfriend~~ ~~best friend~~ those *people* raped her

this poem dresses in women's clothing when no one is home

this poem has broken up two marriages

this poem refuses to pay taxes

this poem went to Thailand for sexual reassignment surgery seven years ago but still dreams of its dick still swinging loudly and often wakes with hand around phantom phallus, crying

this poem is vegetarian but savors the smell of bacon in the air and on her hamburger

this poem only knows how to fake an orgasm

this poem pretended to be homosexual in order to get out of the draft

this poem, smuggled in your pocket, pressed against your thigh, may never understand the existence of god, proper hydration and the necessity to carry more than three condoms at all times

inside the box, there was a calendar. pink plastic cushion with padding called diaper called sanitary napkin called heavy burst of cotton and plastic against vagina like chaperone interruption from underwear fondle. i was fifteen i was twelve i was just past sixteen i was ten. it was so late, i thought body had forgotten me. it was so late i thought body was growing claymation penis made from blood and slaps and ingestion of processed food and excessive sodium that just needed water to grow like chia pet from within. when it came, i searched for bandages big enough to stuff inside me to mop it up. searched for anything to stuff inside me to sop it up. brassieres from sister's dresser, envelopes unclasped with ghost of electric bill final notice form letter jury duty date of appearance. learned foreign language called menstruation called tampons called toxic shock syndrome called smelly ocean called douche it away. two to eight days of this vagina crying blood, thirty-five milliliters or more sometimes less, running away. uterine lining shatters like wine glass against tile it is angry. this blood smells like rust on bicycles like garbage disposal like the rejection of internal. once a month, this body chokes up blood in underwear and rage refuses silence. six pairs of underwear ruined times once a month times twelve in a year equal to seventy-two. i never think that one day this blood will become a bully. graffiti up thighs, change the color of skin, reappraise value, scare body from contact. some months, i let it bleed into a puddle past ankles and grow into a pool with limited access to lap swims or scuba dives. color shifts from strawberry to cranberry to cherry cordial pie to black tar heroin.

part one:

~~GUILLOTINE~~

degree of dark space forty five angled confuse/refuse: compounded

slap x///twenty-fourth letter///against ex///fifth letter plus twenty-fourth///current above former///
vowel+consonant///repeated by equal amounts of apart///and a   part
if x= divisor of curved implement//porcelain percentage to the fifth power/packaged by ziplocked container
of intricate integer///corpse of sixty-two inches climbing into wooden mouth///nails of skin///straining
prepositional fraction///where   ex=mistake///error///oversight in calculations and x=dry ice over blown
glass///enclosing drunk lipstick///stained smoke rings/// take ex///subtract *e*///affix striped face onto
complicated equation omitting parenthetical excuses///excusing unhygienic estimations///

smear   shattered rubber from
flat parchment-inhalation
moment of movement
leaning lending integer
minus one hour for
traveling,   unraveling
green particle of algebraic strand
sitting atop root of
shoulder divided by blade
ur counted 2 x
(m)e   subdivided by
fractioned ellipsis
.../...

where percentage is minimalized by
enlarged compass of firm directions
read:
end   before beginning
conclusion   before hypothesis
black tar trigonometry
curvy, voluptuous geometry
shape of angled knuckles surfing into
independent variable
functioning as alternate for
mast(r) bait *ng*

slick back polynomial
complicated expression eluding
clash of theorems,   where
ex becomes negative like
diagnosed distillation, deconstructing
smoothed out quadratic confusion

sharpen wood with .8 percent of lead

leading to sweetened substitute for   *ex*
additional limbs, concentrated by
subtracted imperfections
multiples of six *i's*
(i) (i) (i) (i) (i) (i)
translated into
forty-five   angled   compounded   equations

Herring glow for a certain period of time after they die.   (Laird Hunt)

she is silvery fish, captured
salt
smoked slippery
a glow

*We do not know what the herring feels. All we know is that its internal structure is
extremely intricate, and consists of more than two hundred bones and cartilages*
     (W.G. Sebold)

she twists tears around
known cartilage
feeds on the surface of
organisms   orgasms
exercised deliberateness

all we know is she breathes
she is breaths
is she breaths or
breathing

she is modified economy
sure of coast,   pattern of
caught and sliced
she sleeps when her light flickers

melancholy is when
she is taken away
harvested for chewing and
bait

the blindness of instrumental elephants
                    ruffians of beauty
un   known   neck   glass

                        migrating flesh furnaces move
                                                    like
syringes of churned implants

sacred disturbance of evening
leaking teeth—
enamel gods of orphan caves

manifest this:
                    dangling blackout

            knitted skin

                    shape for hunters

To go without blinking creates sturdy retinas. He moved from Moldova to Brooklyn and learned the color hot pink. The act of unclimbing thread from hemmed cuffs is much like sex; wrists invert and twist, while everything once neatly pressed grows disturbed. Pigeon of crème fraiche feathers begs for a chicken wing, fried into garbage can. If I don't write about your face, he will succeed in scaring all the words away. There is such a thing as the scent of paper, knees, and numbers. I bent my bed for you. In Rockwell's painting, woman's cheekbones gather his patience. You are sufficient in breast size and hip strength, with obscenely delicious grammar. The point of departure becomes the agreement of remaining alive. I cry after I masturbate because I'm fearful of catching my disease. The identity of purple is found in its rhyme. This disconnected fist maintains proper distance with anus and hand towel. If I took away her medicine, would she remember how to ————? Love over-eats poetry. Sometimes I wish I were straight enough to produce an unplanned pregnancy. Man with salted palms, presses them together and creates weather. But if I don't know who I am, how can you possibly inscribe me? The way she gathers her thickest lip (the bottom one) into her sandwiched mouth makes me forget. A stare, like pulled apart crescents. If I don't write your name in a poem, you will remain knotted into that tree. Andrew. There is only one direction an elbow may bend. He paid me six hundred dollars to watch a sitcom, eat flank steak with slivered onions and fuck. Coconut oil smoothes curled fingers and cracked follicles. The acid melted each dimple away, leaving skin like a rain-soaked window. The push of piano keys unravels melancholy. It looks like graphite had its way with my chin, but nine stitches kept it closed after falling from panic. Every Sunday, she purchases groceries and calls her daughter, then goes back to sleep. I still don't know whom I caught it from.

Upon closer inspection, cancer.

There was a squeeze of posture and nipples.
Her sleep is long-sleeved and lathered.

                    He arrived on a Thursday to spray cupboards and corners.
                        Turned kitchen into coffin for mice and roaches.
                            Thirst leads them toward puddles and death.

From the left, heat arrives like a kiss.
Drip of scald, blister, scar.

            This water tastes of mold, she said.

                    With bass between thighs, she extracts three strings from slumber.
            The sound competes with her belly, which has been left untouched for six days.
                                        She digests music instead.

Suddenly, a leaf is assassinated.
Bullets of rain plunge into its papery skin.
In Autumn time, it is a burial ground.
Hands knit together.
Heels collapse onto moving subway.

Morning commute.

Her throat cannot gather the pills. Curls climb over shoulders and flirt. Between her legs, a fist rises. Outside this window, nudist tree colony. Snow falls, a sweater is built. Cows are calmest when pushed between. Their flesh is best when mood stabilizes. She sketches picture of dislocated fingers. Back begs to be cracked daily. Patches of scalp reveal non-prescribed anxiety. Bagel chews man into round comparison. There is only one way out. Her hearing, shattered by brother's gun. Streaks of water compete with décor. Chin is held up by knuckles. Bending reminds floor to remain clean. Is love in your morning coffee? These two lungs are not identical. She waits for him to flush. Wedding rings hide in their pockets. Cuts heal fastest when in mouths. Winter turns women and men cryophobic.

"Call my wife, call my wife!" he screamed as third rail removed his veins from their hiding place. He had no insurance and hoped its electrical current would surprise his sadness away.

Rubber boots psychoanalyzed the hand-eye coordination of Canadian prisoners. Hair beneath vision is caught on her pearls. They gather the taste of her neck but remind her of linen napkin luncheons and the first man that ever felt her. Hats hide unwashed hair and hairline mistreatment and hair color fading. An unwashed scarf draped over fence leaves a rash on her neck. Fingerless gloves allow her to turn the pages of the novel. How is salt on snow different from salt on soup. Are sidewalks less dangerous to walk over when they are seasoned? Brush teeth with compass in mind; do not forget the northeast. Breath tastes best when mint tangles with the outside wind.

Ninety milligrams of side effects will not remove his lisp. On a Friday, he slathers Federico García Lorca over vocal chords like controlled cologne that reeks of Granada. Calls his tongue a Communist, as it slurs war into his teeth. Beside him, a girl grabs his knee and squeezes an erection off his taste buds. The swelling distracts his s's; suddenly he is cured. She took off her socks and climbed her way through stinging nettle and curious ivy. It was the histamine that took notice of her triangular bones jutting, the pull of skin, the color of cockleshells or plaster. Twenty-minutes later, she brought peeled fingernails toward ankles and itched the irritant away. She was not ready for a relationship at this time. What happened is this. She closed her eyes, which she pretended were moss—not the color but the plant—knees bent in the only way they could and found Braille between her legs. Upon further examination, she attempted amputation. Pink wigged man intrigues red haired lady at basement bathhouse. She drips oiled wax along the seam of his arm, which is veined like skirt steak and dotted with drops of hair. It is his birthday and buttercream-covered penguins decorate his cake. Her pale pink fingers press into his bleached and blotted forearm, his wrist, above his elbow. She nods when he asks her, "Do you like men who dress as women?" She shakes her head when he offers to tie her up like Christmas or roast beef.

Inflation of vessel. Urine's grumble awakes her from bones' hours off. On the way to bathroom, overheard orgasm from shared wall square roots itself. She squats over plumbing. Relief of two beers, processed spit and small bladder turn white water into lemon curd yellow. She does not want to ruin roommate's dramatic sing-along, so a flush is not acted upon this time. On the way back to bedroom, she lingers. Listens to sounds of plunging: plastic-wrapped organ into genetically carved receptacle. This is why beds should be left unslept, she thinks. Or, this is why sheets should stay laundered, she decides. As fingers curve around doorknob, she quietly enters bedroom where her sheets are stained with solitude, two drops of menstrual blood and popcorn kernels from earlier in the night.

He asks if I am Jewish, as I adjust posture in the backseat of fourteen dollar cab ride. His name is Ismael and I tell him yes. His siblings are spread out in Israel, Brazil, New Jersey, Minnesota. He is spread out in one room apartment in Bay Ridge. Your hair is red, he announces, and it feels new and unrealized. Can a Jew not have this color? We exchange recipes for hummus, baba ganoush and Jewish prayer. He speaks to me in Hebrew and I am embarrassed to ask for its translation. Ismael is taxi driver, airport security worker, on his way home after bringing me home. It's my day off, he adds. I just didn't have anything else to do today.

She is unaware that she does this, but when she is ready to let them go, she cuts her hair and they have been together through three trimmings and he has heard about her problem and has hidden all the scissors, razors and knives sharp enough to slice through bangs and split ends and she suddenly notices his stutter and the way that he wears his socks until payday they grow sweaty by the toes and at night after they fuck he licks her shoulder because it is salty, but no other place on her body gets this kind of lapping and when he eats he slurps his peas and soda cans sit on counter tops with bendable straws because he injured his neck when he was driving before she met him and he pours corn syrup on his pancakes and chicken fried steak and he never wears collars or colors and suddenly her scalp is itchy, hungry for a thinning, a fade, perm or highlight enhancement and at night she watches him watch her twirl it between her fingers and push it into her mouth and gag.

Four days past her birthday, Esmeralda gets a spanking. Leather skirted, zipper crotch and he lifts her over his lap. Skirt rises as red fabric encloses the seam of her bum and he places flat palm over her. Her master, out of town until Saturday, will compete with the wallops when he returns. He leaves before her bedtime and arrives far beyond her morning tea. Around her neck, a collar snaps into place waiting for his leash to pull her back in again. She says *thank you* after each slap, before each gasp, after spectators spot the coloring of her skin. She thinks of beautiful women wearing her fingers, slightly wrinkled, like an article of clothing. Twenty-five or thirty-two lashings because the counter lost count and Esmeralda can handle it. She never speaks of the man's rise beneath his own leather which is just below her belly and she never speaks about the first time she saw this man with elephant trunk of man inside his mouth and feather duster sweeping up his insides and she never speaks about the first time she was spanked when she was six because it did not feel quite like this. She rises as skirt plummets down toward center of thighs and her loose skin falls back into place. She smiles big gap between teeth and red lips worn down from kissing in corners and sipping on cranberry and seltzer. A redhead calls her stunning and sexy and she no longer feels the sting. She grabs small hand of woman with dimples and they find each other's waist and they kiss. Several generations split between them, yet hands go in similar places and their tongues never touch but lipstick exchanges placement from Esmeralda's to another.

Burnt fist finds comfort in groan. What assumption may b found from scarf wick? Find crumbling rust lust on math dripping against lips. Do you stand? Sip crust of paintbrush. Bottom of stain may show exhaust strip. In book, obtain brain of corn root. Pinpoint history of warts. Bump against hula-hoop with hips. Construct windows from hair. Family transforms mold through distraction. Sink blood prompts woman to pay bills on occasion. How do fish multiply? Why must intimacy drag a body past its comfort? Moist mama must marry prior to giving birth. No. Knots of translation flock into church. God births story with rhythmic chant. Child absorbs guilt from holy book. Follow along with drugs and unknown virus. Snort snails up nostril or dollar bills. Do not justify starvation, worship, and fiction. Gut a pig for lunch and only touch its snout. Can you afford to kiss? Hug my last wrist. What big gulps you stash on your wound. Why blood sways forward built from bricks of human. Sing as though you vanish skin. Without paint or pain or pupils. Commit globalization or turn into a communist or farmhand. Organic fruit has a tart flavor. That Canadian with blond whisps of hair walks six blocks for warm milk and a flax muffin. Wish thighs could talk? May sound Yiddish or worn out. Dad cannot afford socks or plastic bags. How his hurt transforms into infirmity. Nothing is factual, minus absorption of panting. Blown out cavity tricks flavor. Hospital drum falls from grid of furry doorway; its knob rough from curry rub. Catch sound of harpsichord clinging to chair lift. Dollars cost most on Sundays; why is that? Malnourish cups of cocoa dust or sarcastic quotation marks. In the room, knitting of stitched confusion. A foraging fork thinks about spoons. Toward Virginia Woolf quotation, "For most of history, anonymous was a woman." Talk to touch humanity. Chant truths on a Thursday in a room built from coin thrusts and copulation. Pay it forward to film constructor or photograph originator. Black and gray contraption. Toward guitar, strumming a folk stitch. Spool sits on body and unsnarls starvation. Basis of assassination: forlorn. Cook asparagus, garlic, carrot and broccoli, slow and low. Unborn child calls out ultimatum using partial palms against familiar tummy. Hours arriving as thumbnails on mountaintops drop fat onto highway. Glass lit stars push into sky of brick yawns. It is a cold diagnosis; waxy cotton winds music against sick. Drink milk from pillows or tattoos and join circus. Laugh about clouds, vinyl suits, rainy lipstick, or painful burst of dirt into traumatic scar. Do not throw cork away. Find family uniformity in mirrors or shortcomings. Awkward pupil cannot contain focus. Laugh at tourists conducting back-flips against boundary crossings. The bravado of sprouts fondling soil. Warmth for pork sparks hostility from holy sanctuary.

We must throw away the color pink. Gather black skinned garbage bag with built in yellow handles. Press air inside to reveal capacity of space. Born in seventeenth century, this pigment called girl lacks genitals. Blushed portrait called flower. Derived from crinoline and china patterns, hair bows and high heels. Hold her down and remove her orgasm. Remove her motherhood. Push cartilage and bends into hair and tie her pout into knots. She walks hollow. Clutches eye lashes to cheeks. Squeezes away genes of paternal, country, pain of infection. Dressed as mutilation, autistic father uses scalpel as compressor. Speaks in incomplete sentences when between her thighs, removing her pink. Scissors blink her away. Gender is best received in a question mark.

ab   NORMAL
one hundred sit-ups per day   FLATTENS THE IT AWAY

: call me deviation.   .,<} /\| 00---{}

inter   SEX
between legs a fist rises   MUTINY

: when (I) was six, (I) tore out a section of my neck where the label sat. where the label rubbed. where the label pushed pink where there was yellow. where the label reconstructed [my] structure. where the label took away sensation. where the label told {me} how to pee. where the label disguised {me}. Discussed {me}. DISgusts {me}.

inside on the   OUTSIDE
there is outside   INSIDE

: understand this need to disfigure/wires wind within notarized parts of gender serration/scribble/inscribe/take notes against the flesh that fondles omission/a blunder?/illustrate the in-between/a multiple choice of organs and identities/divide gender into name/hair style/occupied paycheck/cancel out what remains

:micro penis.   instru/MENtal

small formation like   INDECISION
color will cure it   FOR NOW

*: sensations are not acceptable/inaccessible/the swelling/swallowing/(I) looked {me} up
in the book of explanations and found*

                                              graffiti'd pout/magnification of gen.i.tals

morph   OLOGY
bi   OLOGY
gender is not   SEX

*:doctor gave {me} a passport to cross the border of this body/man in badges and nametag
stopped {me} at the fringe of internal & external/pouring of salt to/preserve* IT */melt*
IT */embarrass* IT *away*

:she/he/she/he/she/he/   ititititititititititititititititititititititititititit

                  [fuck]

ambiguous   to doubt   debate   vague   (a) lie.

        : just   *call*   *me*   *a*   *question*   *mark*

nudity is not enough to keep the sweat away   at night, blankets huddle over body
and attempt impregnation   and so it begins   flirtations with yeast and
pinot noir   non-organic poses   elbows reflect tabletop to head ache
starvation of shadows   ankles   earlobes   gather posture   prescriptions
notice of distension   *there is a lot about me you don't know*   flirt of leg
hair   collision of straps   a crescent   a scar   a numerical remainder
division is every where   her clit is a foreign country   classically trained
pelvis   shivered clench of furrows   castration of nudity
for research   *recognize this madness?*   *mother gave it to me on my twelfth
birthday*   preserve trauma   energy   plastic wrapped tongue
beauty recognized by repeat performances   stab comfort zone   a splinter
distension   analysis of medication   currency of envelopes   *it only
counts if he comes*   the mention of laps   straddle of earth worms
slide of her half-eaten apple   connection of the tiptoe   *believe this*
take the blur out   binge on history   segregate the pretty ones   eye
lids clean odor from constant flapping   courage of confession   *he ran it
into me*   what remains has rotten   pink is not a color   it is an affliction
a witness   pay at the door   wipe feet inside   wash hands with soap-
shaped muscle   forget
she is a woman   was a woman   tucked away   *the poverty of sex*
an unlocked door   bare feet   a weapon   experiment with sound
cracking   a shove   impolite fist   *her narrative reeks contradictions*
an animal with skin losing   looseness   weight of extinction
elephants walk toward the moisture   a swallow of appropriate organs *I
want to jump off the ledge of this body*   and die   before the wet is
found

protist1 gender4	protist1 gender12
lenses[x] seam ripper[ծ] comb[ı] a climb ticker tape[ɛ] sex: singular/plural hair[ɪ]	abstraction of intention role play devolution[η]
protist1 gender7	protist1 gender17
to run swallow sit on be (sit on) kiss without lips involved[ι]	lichen-like[ɜ] secrets[ı] madness[ʌ] starvation[μ] monsterism[ϕ]

---

[x] vision from behind glass or plastic/what it means to notice/blue nailed girl on subway sits behind leather knees and cries three oceans against prescription/how much should one be forced to take in/are we all guilty of accepting money/   /passports not needed to exploit the feminine/she sits beside you/sleeps against your erection/i am the I it/I/

[ծ] itch of tenderized/plow of particles/purchase woman.girl.holes/men in hard hats dig at pavement-skin/to create stronger surface/paid by government/   /place metal phallus against black top and vibrate against the hardness/ road is smooth now/drive over it/see for yourself/why is this permitted/

[ı] knots cling to the knuckles of bedsheets/snow forms without winter present/flakes of body/dirt/drugs/ pigment/hair/

[ɛ] constant flow of words/there is meaning found in the neon/read fast/there is no time to repeat/she tells her story to microphones and analysts/tells her story to prescription pads and bar stools/blows nose in scar tissue/grows shell over exposures/writes poems to understand the why/

[ɪ] there is preference for smooth skin/silk of childhood/they do not want to interact with hair/now, she forces fur to cover places that have been breathed against/pushed into/rubbed away/taken/   /

[η] three stages of syphilis/room for personalized shame/blisters appear as mouth bubbles/experienced fullness/swell from the friction/from forgotten questions/more money is made when less protection is worn/

[ι] does cancer have a smell/   /does herpes have a taste/   /does hpv live rent free on taste buds that taste her/that purchase her parts for harm/   /do lips imprint each time they gather mouth chap/   /tongues are muscles that can break or burst or lift or/   /he left four of his cavities inside/   /she cannot be kissed/there/

[ϕ] slowly IT grows/another gender to take the place of the one that has been taken/she hides behind woven tree tops/climbs toward height of bridges/to jump is to confess there is nothing left/is nothing left/is nothing left?/   /a simple, slow-growing plant/a simple,   slow-slumping   body/the   moist   of   her   past/   mildewed   female/when   one gender/identity/breast/clit/belly/thigh/hip/elbow/freckle/dimple/eyelash/ bend/thumb/earlobe/is stolen/there is need to find an other/

[ɜ] my mother sold me to men that did not want her/my father left too early/I was raped/I was given too many hallucinogens for supper/I was curious, so I let him pay me for sex I might not have given away/I liked it sometimes/it is easier to be promiscuous and call it a job/he crept in my room at night when I was nine/I was stolen/IT was stolen/they were just filling up all the parts of me that had been emptied and hollow/

[ʌ] hereditary/caught/transferred/given to the youngest child/

[μ] pills save time from jaws/the chew of teeth/the swallow/there is already enough to spit/food remains in bottles and body/parts/rib caged/breast boned/cunt coughs/sickness becomes/only family member to remain

[ϕ] what happens when water runs out and sex cannot be rubbed away

Arrived at the terrain of her sensibility[1]

red dot   painted in the middle of constructed black fibers
call(ed) herself a parking garage
throw away
bed sheets
ailment

bred herself
sores and stains
discourse for journalists, poets, feminists
misery for her mother   (*of* her mother)

lifted each foot as though
as though
as though they were hands lifting her toward
toward
better

welcome
define
speak

think of poem

women cross borders
pushed over borders

chained energy
window'd enclosure [   ]

it is by choice they breathe
but moans are pressurized
debt extractors

New York Chicago Toronto Vancouver
Turkey Israel Thailand Bangledesh
Hong Kong   Macedonia
right here   right here

---

[1] all text in italic taken from Barbara Guest's, "A Reverie on the Making of a Poem"

traffic patterns of women's
flesh   burns   fright

struggle

and when she was finally able to masturbate
tears replaced cum

how can she touch what no longer exists?

balance and non-movement
preparation
force in poem

want her to look like a woman
like with tight dressing
like with heeled high clinked walking
like with long hair
like flowy
like clean

want her to look like she likes it
like looooooong moans
like across the room ejaculation
like body remaining awake after ten men in
sixteen hours

with no warning (from inside the text,
mind attached to the text).

and you still want to touch this?

In the attack of suspense:

sound of the last words—
echo

most common strand sewing these women
men
women
together

no one wants to admit it

admit it
admit it

       (i) am one of you

                   destructiveness
                    Countdown!

nine hundred thousand
eight hundred thousand
women
men
children trafficked across borders

                With a fist held loftily—
                 Muscular control

when skin peeled
new cells swelled over gaps

                  take chances
             motion, movement in poem

an
   investigation
           of
    seven teen   genders
              to/ get/ her
    packed and in   and out

               of this

GET OUT OF MY BODY

movement coalescing
with the strict idea

fondle door knobs and see what happens
when he opens the door, spit in his face
grab weapon of mass construction and
bend away
redefine sex gender beauty birth rights freedom refusal   SURVIVAL

there is need for binding. to strap parts down that have been misplaced, mishandled, misunderstood. to place make-up on parts that are malnourished, malleable, monsterized. to channel first love and think of her/him/them. when being fucked by strangers, creatures, owners. to forget where home is. Moldova. Tel Aviv. Mother's womb. Orphanage. New Jersey. A home. Room. Closet. To understand the why: too poor, too pained, language barrier, body barrier, abuse, rent, for passport, for family, for food, for drugs, to exist…

INDEX

begin in a place with no end

ask   because no one knows they should

wait   because there is a promise her innards will speak

now   because history grows sore on her feminine and there needs to be a
remedy

the next morning she woke up and spoke, "The most dangerous parts of me."

gathered belongings: thighs, fragmented collarbone, cleaved lips, fingerprints, clumps of
hair, dangling clitoris, breasts almost hauled off body, nightmares, the leftover pills, one
pair of underwear without hem or elastic, a needle bent and bleeding, three bandages
without adhesive, a condom, extra sweater soiled and weary, loose change offering music
while the clank of existence hums

her name is daughter
at fifteen, she replaced chewing with swallowing

the rain came

wind pushed against her bruises
too late for a sex talk

and then

a climb toward her highest window. she could not afford a security system so

there was breaking when he entered

skin grows resistant to carpet threads against kneecaps
push of circumcised erection against unclaimed cavity

open up, open up, open up, open up. everyone laughs when discomfort is felt.

now

talk about the time he   when he cut   called whore   loaded infliction inside
and

talk about the time he   all doors locked and your bag was   he said he would blur
out your face and only show   parts for purchasing

talk about the time your mother approached you like a business owner
"I made you," she said. "I gathered you for nine months. Now…

give.it.away

                "

smoked cigarettes delivered in his mailbox
stroked the cancer that lay benign in his groin
slept against the indentation his wife made in king-sized mattress
swept up reticence while he stole several slices of her being

several months later,

drank orange juice and threw it down her throat to gag his tongue away

and then

he said "It is because of men like me that women like you exist."

he said "You don't act *gay*. I can tell you like it."
she envisioned his small penis as an oversized clit and bit down on her imagination

he wanted to feel small, so she stepped on him...................................... $75[v]

GFE.. $150

Bareback.. $50+

Blood play.. $80+

Knife Play.. $120+

Open mouth kissing... $45+

Punching, Spitting... $40
(sometimes complimentary)

Shaving, Hair pulling, Choking.. $30

Sleepover... $650

Various Excrements.. $100+

Humiliation.. $60+

To be entered and exited without question without pause without without......$$$

$$$=It can be difficult to move away from the monetary value of an action

enter   analysis

---

[v] U.S. currency

[*] girlfriend experience

It is different when you are white   when you have a mailbox and home to hide in
when your water is turned on and there is soap to suck on   when you can stop if you
really want to   it is different when you start to tell people and they ask if you liked it
did you fake it   what does your boyfriend think   husband   what do you mean
you're *queer   trans   gender?* was it painful   and they ask, was it fun   and they ask,
did they make you feel good   did you *feel* good   do you feel   ?

the men never ask what book she is reading or   if she voted for the right person or
her stance on war or

she just wanted to know what it would feel like to be feminine:
pigment of wax   hair inching past shoulders   distance from floor to feet
lace

so the women are introduced to photographers and journalists
documentarians
feminists and poets
fetishists

someone recognizes her from when she

the next day, she decides to stop
a reverse strip-tease

then,

the qualms of her uterus struck by instrumentation of karma

a warrant for the arrest of her health

after the scraping, bill collection, humiliation of straddled odorous complaint
she pushes by-the-hour pussy back together   and
weeps

suddenly,

she misses the instability of her body

one last time   she whispers

because she cannot remember what happened the last time
because infection arrives once and then it lays dormant
because boredom is worse than being breathed against by strangers
because she worries she likes it

The next day, she sits at a desk and flirts with silence. She breaks a muscle in her thigh from clenching her right and left together. Then, she was asked to read a poem. She was asked to make supper. She was expected to balance a checkbook. She was forced to fuck five men in a span of four hours. She was pushed against bricks and asked to smile even when the blood escaped. She was persuaded to use her cunt as a cabinet; with limited space, the objects just kept falling out. She was mistaken for a human. She was kissed as though her lips were clean. She was held. She was burned.

oh, and then there is this

to be kissed with instrumental mouth

to be asked   *may I continue*

to be told   *beauty exists where trauma ends*

an attempt at love

begin with the sound of envelopes unlatching   no, a mother unclasping sanity from
forearms and cigarette-distracted teeth   or when uncle hugged her so hard the sound
of tearing became familiar   and the first inhale of stimulants   or when she was
told masturbation was a crime, so she was already a criminal   wait: she began inside
a body and continues the burden of entrapment

Her important parts are blurred. On a Saturday, she will gag her mouth borrowed from her mother with panty hose borrowed from her roommate. She will use industrial rope borrowed from hardware store during its busiest time to tie herself up like stack of newspapers on curbside. Black braided rope will twist between breasts size small because she is still saving, over belly, flat like roadkill on highways, between lips of vagina so clit can have its fifteen minutes of stardom. Boston bread brunette contemplated the nunnery. Moved to New York to collect library loans and leather shoes. Quits job after paycheck turns blank. Boston bread brunette becomes a nanny, housecleaner, ghostwriter of term papers, foot fetish model. Her toes spread like bacteria from an open sneeze. When they ejaculate on her arch, she thinks about Hemingway, de Beauvoir and Joyce. Woman from exit eleven off the turnpike tells him that the scars distracting her arms are from sex. Tells her that the scars were an art project when she ran out of paper. Tells them she had a rough time accepting adolescence. Woman from exit eleven off the turnpike collected staples from magazines, safety pins holding her hem in, razorblades removed from plastic pink razor. Her flesh formed into bandages. Scabs resembling inchworms, bleeding. She tried to scratch her self away.

He took off his wedding ring before entering purchased woman

Your breasts are humorous. That place on that street where those people purchased things to force away their troubles has closed due to the economy. The woman took too many pills and scarred her thighs and that man hung himself in the basement. Daughter is a verb. Outside, pigeons place scalps into puddle of snow. Garbage floats in the water like abandoned kayaks. I can smell her today: masculine breath, beer and childhood. He calls his father by his first name. For instance, her womb scares itself. For example, the hanger was made of plastic and too smooth to scrape. Giraffes symbolize ~~foreskin~~ foresight of the Egyptians. I painted my car orange, so parking lot does not lose it. I should have painted my mother too. She was carried away in a suitcase, body bent like the straw used to suck up her last meal.

Spray-painted on brick wall before train goes back below, "Get out of art school. You are beautiful." Someone rubs the second "T" away on sign and suddenly wet paint turns into suffering. He gathers interest in woman who shifts seats on subway. Student loans gather on lap to afford canvas, paint and a purpose. Drizzled chemicals cause the cracks to run away from walls. Her body heat forces him to take off one of his coats. She slams her flesh into fibers after lathering acrylic over pores. Someone left a name inside the stain before it dried. He smells his fingers, disappointed by his lack of washing and care. Evaluate art by its level of confusion. There is a kiss against sign, which crumbles in the corners from shoulders. He gathers the measurements of her face by not blinking. Sounds of train remind her of oil and brush strokes. He slips one or three fingers into her and removes the other "T". She looks like his mother and his zipper begins to rub against his memory. She waits to call herself an artist until they hand her the diploma.

A liver fasts inside swollen. Body begs fingers to leave it. Alone, she waits by the closed portion of her door in case he. Returns can be made within seven. Days are only complete if they end in anonymous. Fucking is an action that often ends in debilitating. Illnesses do not wait for a more convenient. Time removes the hairs on his. Wrists can be turned into paper snowflakes, cut up and. Hung by a belt that came with green shorts that no longer fit. Waist grabs onto his hands or his hands grab onto her. Waste exits a body after a night of slammed happy. Hour twelve of the day yields a sandwich made from tomatoes, lettuce and. Mayonnaise can be used as lubricant when the real stuff runs. Out, before you know who I

Do something wrong, he says as fingers wipe themselves into beard longer than an inch but shorter than a mile. His third button got lost somewhere between Manhattan and Brooklyn or washing machine and drawer. Places tongue between lips while plastic bottle enters mouth and filtered water falls into him. Not so good sex is much better than no sex at all, he adds. Distracted by cooking, recipes of stories and a beautiful man who has read three books in his lifetime. Fifty thousand limbs inside his mouth, against his mouth, inside, into, in, out, in out. Pen in left pocket and crooked over teeth. Three silver circles pierce left ear as white hair like fourth day city snow covers the rest of him. Daughter tried to take his words away, which keep him steady until he collapses. He is vanilla, hand-holding, pressing of body into partner of twenty-one years. Speaks of monogamy as an allergy or a game people play like religion. Makes you twist yourself up into some bizarre monster or a misery like adult-onset chicken pox or dieting. He is an isolationist, not contortionist, but Marxist. At 4:30am, he rises without alarm or sounds other than body creaking over mattress. Cane knocks against floor as he pushes weight into morning. Words never stop coming. He never stops coming. When there is nothing left to write, he makes breakfast.

She balances left foot against calf of right. There is a shifting of fabrics that appear to include glitter, flame-retardant chemicals and the fingerprints of young babies paid pennies per pant leg. Ceramic bowl sits on counter top just washed with hot water and paper towel. Grapefruit in white webbed skin rests in her palm. She is pink-haired dancer with appetite for pungency and rind. She removes the sour from thin casing, places ripped flesh into bowl. Between bites, she speaks about feminism, hair length and the need to identify as sloppy versus *put together*. Each bite bursts the wedge of citrus wide open. Her teeth are sprayed with its tart ejaculate. It is lunchtime. She will chew and swallow for eight more minutes between conversational interludes. Then, she will walk toward bedroom wearing socks and lips still red from the night before, close her door and sing.

Red zipped sweater hides apology of two pimples placed eloquently on skin like a racial slur. He celebrates girlfriend named Linda, dressed in purple crushed poems and lips painted red. They sit beside one another like mismatched articles of clothing. His tongue is too big for his body. His tongue is too small for her body. Her hands leave a mark on his knee like an oil spill. Letters lunge out of his mouth before proper spell-check or grammar exchange. Sneakers expose his inability to tie a proper knot as large strip of velcro eases his feet into a safely tightened composure.

Takes bow and arrow and beer can and poem and homosexual hiding spot and polyester suit and scuffed shoes and socks with enough holes in them to call them dish rags and eyewear that he decides to take off so that he does not see her wince and aims at her forehead. He takes pills and penises into mouth and does not chew before swallowing. He lives in cabin of horizontal wood and cast iron pans and kerosene slow burn beneath the weight of cooking. Hallucinates bodies and abstinence as streets hold his legs up while heroin pays for his morphine. Fled to Mexico, fled jail, fled sanity, fled Paris, fled withdrawal, fled the church of scientology. He purchased highs from outside his front door, from lower east side, from mourning, in the morning. Moved to Kansas to live and die and fish and shoot and breathe without intrusion. Heart failed him at six fifty pm when the sky was getting darker and eighty-three years became his limit.

apostrophes are meant to signify the formation of teardrops against construction paper. she speaks about the rhythm of politics, gender and the need to repeat. she is mother, boulder, poet, daughter, she is braided, school of disembodied poetics, she is lost, absent, gone now. *tell me what you see while I stay to miss you.* activist without pretense, she defined feminism as action, inclusion, storm of words quietly raging between spine. she is teacher, performer, lover, friend, sister, she is brooklyn, focused stare, she is memory. light grieves for you as it sets its flame down and honors your need to go.

---

* Dan Dissinger

avoid blue   careful hyphen   mug vitamin   sip burn

mental coat   pull son   portrait snow   tree able

mosaic whine   tissue death   chew ephemeral   knit rock

umbrella speak   lean asleep   knee cord   guilt range

bench brow   thread crawl   ceramic indent   envelope undress

Hassidic boys play hide-n-go-seek as facial hair holds mouth and cheeks hostage. On a Thursday, after prayer bows and god memorization, father travels downtown on 3 train then B train toward basement. Man called Ron in sparkles and leopard print, recognizes his fetish and sends him toward the back. Hassidic man in Hassidic beard and peyes and tzitzit traveling past his waist, and black fedora hiding his eyes, shyly gathers the women. Dom named Krisella whips his clothes off his body, the scent of unwashed satin and perspired guilt. He says *amen* each time she beats him. Calls out *amen* as she rips the grey out of his beard and places the curls over his tongue. He sings out the prayer for absolution as she rubs her leather over his circumcised religion, ties him up and leaves him.

the cutting of. [preferable female]^^
language. /no: o. o. o.   o. o.   **o.o.**   o. o. no. no.   no.no.no.no.no.no.no.no.

tone the *IT* down

memory. [popping] trauma. [visceral] [absorption]
neuter. wounds. [pussy]   Cut.

[his intelligence is a mere tool in the service of his drives and needs]

size can be challenging
disappointing   and a relief.

prescribed hard-on   lasts longer than agreed upon   envelopes crammed with
Presidential love
letters   a doorman   athletic semen   running

[despising] [loneliness] [without the aid of males] Up. [touching gold] [milk] [scum]

alkaline solution
grease of animals
glycerol, crude
purification not enough
wash the IT away

[non-human] trembled serration clings to parenthetical scars

[a biological accident] [incomplete]
[the refuge of the mindless]

---

^^ text in brackets cut up and mutilated from SCUM Manifesto by Valerie Solanas

severing the [grotesque]. breaths. wrists. clit. [bread]. yeast. [scum].
[machine].

[adapted themselves to animalism]

                                   cock   cuh/cuh/uh/uh/c-c-c-c-c-c-c-uh-uh-under-under

[a place] [in the slime]
trapped under the IT

[constantly seeking out] specification
[barely perceptible physical feeling]

tore out cunt during reconstructive phase
now all that remains is   an echo

                                        [SCUM is impatient]

                                                          ! ...

the pauses must be removed because there is no time to gasp/   too much to take in
now

can be found beneath sinks
sodium hypochlorite
gags stains
disinfectant
burns facial gestures and nasal passageway
bleach

                              not   {strong}   enough.

codification of the IT:

    I.   serrated gender
        a. [incomplete set of] [emotional]
        b. saw tooth distance between groin and
        c. the inside of an outside or outside of an inside

    II.   accidental [X]
        a. mistaken for boy by father
        b. mistaken for girl by doctor
        c. mother always wanted a girl, so

    III.   in other words
        a. erroneous
        b. misdirected
        c. mistaken
        d. monsterism

or,   [a walking abortion] [peddling] [asses] [love(s)] [substitute]

Valerie,

Our skin is from New Jersey. Our mothers smell of stainless steel and ECT.
Lacerations linger against hips from rent payment. Pop artist pretended to get
you. *Get you. Get you.* I *got* you, Valerie. I see your leather. Typewriter inked
kneecaps. Leaning. The lunge of exhausted hate. I was there but. Different room
but. Different bed but. Different men but.   *I*   *was*   *there.*

I would tear out my cunt and give you mine just so you could fondle
decontamination.*

*there is no such thing.

He begins to remove his tie. The beautiful agony of a knot carefully constructed, folded over buttons. The way he inhales his cigarette makes her long to be an addict. When his neck becomes undone, he pushes his shirt away. Close-up of tongue gathering the fibers of paper and fire, a Parisian kiss of sucked in tobacco. He requests to see her naked and when she declines, he becomes restless. Lead me to your bookshelf, she says. *Les Fleurs du Mal* climbs into his hands. *Ham on Rye* climbs into hers. I will show you my wrist, she announces. An oval of skin, with nicked creases comes into contact with small camera attached to computer frame. He squints his eyes to read the word tattooed over her scars. Her lips get licked each time she is turned on or nervous or gathering loose coffee dripped away from mouth. There is a small death each time we orgasm. Each time our muscles lose composure and tighten like bricks pulled together by concrete. This is called an execution. A massacre in the body upon improperly exposed climax. I miss your tie, she exclaims. There is a removal of three fingers from inside her vagina, as he begins to loosely strangle his neck again. He doesn't notice her placing those fingers into mouth, sucking out her orgasm before she clicks him away.

You don't know what it's like to be finger fucked. I buried all the hairs beneath rubble of skin and on the day of the night of seeing her speak, my uterus fell out. *Let me piss in your mouth.* I walked seventy blocks in search of a store that sold some kind of spoon or shovel to dig it out of me, and then it just fell. *You wish you had a clit, but you only have a cock.* She was pushed on a Monday by white boys with white hair and white cells and white words and she only gets up now to do yoga. *Suck my suck my suck my...* Her breakfast looked much better as purged digestion against ring of unwashed toilet breath. *I want your wiener in my mouth.* My left breast is slightly smaller than my right and I wonder if you notice and if you do please keep it to yourself. *I've got Belgium waffles in my twat.* So many portraits of women watching themselves in the mirror; before purchasing, we need to check for warping. *I'm swimming in piss.* The mountains allowed her enough space to mourn the poet who had been missing who had been mourning who is mourned. *I'm going to shit in your ears.* I can schedule in a suicide on Wednesday after five but not before because I'm having lunch with a prospective client or having my teeth cleaned or workshopping a poem, but after that, I have plenty of time to practice death.

---

* All text in italics cut up from Karen Finley's mouth

a play, of sorts
or
a need to disrobe to satisfy rental agreement
and
two-tiered body dressed in cocaine and homework
or
the year she lived inside men

[*note: body, interruption, translation* and *direction may be read by second or third voice.*
hu/man and form may be read by female or of unknown gender. when cues are given, allow enough
pause for action or movement to take place.]

[hu/man walks up to plugged in skinny mouth with holes and wires and rubber grip. microphone
may be used as a substitute]

                              [body]
                              tremble
                              [pause]
                              informal deception
                              [show]
                              nudity may be required or   hidden
                              [cue disrobe]

                              [interruption]
                              acoustics is a word we cannot afford
                              make your teeth scream

hu/man: why must there be a beginning?
        confessions create silence, but maybe
        I long for neglect or dis
        regard

[form]
do not make eye contact.
do not approach the scars.
do not fall in love.
if there is mention, there will be denial.
look in,   like store-front window or rearview mirror
use kindest, loneliest finger to understand origin of why skin is raised
kiss   like lips excrete unfiltered water as gasped tongue responds to clarity
there is a need to tell this, so gather a befitting audience

hu/man: she poured baby powder on my toes and watched its
          albino shadow disrupt the wooden floors.
        he placed his erection against me like an awkward wool sweater,
         itchy and disruptive.
          she kissed me when she ran out of men and interest.
        they watched when drugs no longer circulated; sex became last remaining source.
         she mistook words for paper plates, messy and bent; they all got thrown away.
        he admired the length of her orgasm and the distance between her no's and mouth.
        they pretended not to notice when she leaked tears from her vagina.

[body]
create the shape of a bridge
collapsing

[interruption]
begin long stretch of uncomfortable
contact
use stare, tips of fingers, selection of
taste buds
do   not   let   go—wait.

talk about the time you
kept it in your mouth
talk about the time you
ran out of soap;
you kissed her
still smelling of currency and cum
talk about the time you
were photographed
head removed, clit exposed
talk about the time you became inflamed
talk.about.the.time.

hu/man: when do we first learn how to swallow?
       is it understood or
    might it be a trained response of first nipple in mouth
    the milk that floats out of it
    what we must do to keep
    from choking.

    when do we yearn?
    in what moment can we define?

[interruption]
ssssshhhhhhhh.
she is getting softer.

[form]
pillow placed between
pre-teenaged thighs thirsts upon
surprised sensation

[trans/lation]
the first time she masturbated,
she understood the power of
deliberate touch

[direction]

look away   ashamed
interpret the body language of sin

[body]
slow   ly   fall
or sway to suspend
conversion

hu/man: all that is left to say I write.

[interruption]
pause

the language of bedsprings
of elbows bent awkwardly and kneecaps rubbed off
of childhood reenacted in moans and fixed-rate humping
the need to entertain, to be seen, misunderstood or just
missed
hiding behind metaphors and english and therapy
inhalation of trauma
exhalation of puncture wounds

[body]
reveal disfigurement or
lick   wrist

[direction]
wait
for understanding
to form[1]

---

[1] length of time uncalculated, reward of complete transliteration to those who remain.

why must there be a beginning?

cunt's tree   climbs boneless   step ladder   and carnival of pushing

huh.uh.huh.uh.uh.uh.

womb stink
daughter malignancy
marination of convenient religion

heterosexual health insurance
wrapped up tiny blond ring on
smoker's coughing finger

[immunization Nation]

two months off of breast:
dietary resuscitation

New Jersey, crooked leg
gateway drug

shivering

rolling pinned eyes at seventeen
Jennifer from the movie theater
Jennifer from the mental hospital
Jennifer between legs and sucking out   posture

Ernst Gräfenberg from fingertips
contractions contortions   musical accompaniment

exit exchange from eleven to somewhere north

bleeding ramen broth from lips where disease   touched
unabridged sphincter digesting paycheck

                                        there must *be a why*

loaned student
.08 second intervals of   forgetful

[subsequence

There is a reason to be left. When birth is given, she flees due to malnourished motherhood. After the push, she lost focus. Love is only felt on a Tuesday when the weather is congruent to mood and the phone connection is palpable and there is nothing else better to do than talk on the phone. No, I can't hear you. Hands clasp around face called mouth and leg wraps beneath other called other. To speak, he must place his finger up against his throat to suck in enough air toward his lungs to give him sound. The blood pressure medicine took away his erection and created a wind strong enough to curve him toward the right. On a Friday night, I crept into my bedroom and wept until my nose bled, until the salt water scratched my cornea or *I* scratched my cornea and my walls no longer smelled like you.

Pollack knew exactly where his paint would run off.

Husband knows exactly what his fist will run into.
When she speaks in high-pitched scream she is asking for it.

When he mixes blue and yellow into something like grass stains or leaves,
he is asking for it.
The composition of light against dark and drip against smear is illuminating.

The light against her dark eye once hazel now black and blue and grey and
there appears to be blood in the corners illuminating her swell.

The safe word is no, but when she screams it,
there is no repeal of movement from curled knuckles against squinted face.

There is no safe way to end, but when he screams out done,
there is no stopping his paintbrush.

There is a hole in the wall like enflamed pore over skin where he watches. She knows this, so before bed, she licks her ankles, each elbow twice, bites her bottom lip because he paid extra for that and does not permit her blood to be sopped by tongue, instead, it paints her chin. A different *she* poses for the tree outside her window. In less than three hours, a different *he* will steal the privacy from her bedroom and unfasten the blanket tucked beneath her. He will climb in as though her bed exists a higher altitude. He will combine his weight and hair with hers. Another *her* crunches both eyes shut while another *he* places clothespins called pinchers on her belly like a skirt of lifted skin. She lets go of pain as he treats the wooden clips as a fence and jumps over. Her breath, stolen and tense, flies around her bedroom, plasters the peeping toms hiding on the other side of each wall.

dressed as mutilation,   autistic father uses scalpel as compressor
carving out clitoris of daughter, aged twenty-four months.

ocean of sky wraps swan smeared clouds over flesh folded tiny hood of   genitals pull
petals from   under developed flower:
how much does he love her? let grammatical pronoun count definitive tenderness.

protector of purity challenges expiration date:
curdled bacteria grows   like thoughts in petri dish
african stains   throw glass   into disposal of mouth   hiding between small legs, joints
~~severed~~ seductive.

illegal instrument of power: prototype of male,
throws formation of rock into [against] through   unfinished girl
infected tear ducts   leak   when burnt feminine   perforates.

purple herb corrodes pink gummy birth found in   southern region of georgia
graded heat curved by interception of fire   smothering loins   tender   mopped by
janitor,   breath of ammonia spit into mouth of   child: mute
citizen   of   umbilical cord.

potential conviction of two thousand eighty weeks   not equal to amputated
fertility.   crescent eyes color of   mothers womb, still: squeezed pale pupils
dilated   before scissors act as blinking.

I. A climb into color.

Call her charcoal. Second layer of earth after gardening sheers tear weeds away and worms skate out like slippery strands of dust. What gathers beneath fingernails and covers knuckles. Call her this. Soil. Dark brown. Coffee grounds, not the morning-blend but Guatemalan or Sumatra. Call her thunderstorm. When night exchanges day for purpley tint like first day bruising. Call her this. Call her beat-down. Call her whore as jazz and blues thread themselves over skin and the mood is right for coins and objectification. Her husband may arrive wearing two fists and built-up childhood beatings. Left hand against her right eye and a swell. Scream out putty skin. Pliable ass wears cultural significance of bending. The wipe of men away from black bones. Call her beautiful before pushing her against spackle and unswept floor. Grab hair, twist around sausage fingers and break off roots from greased-up scalp. Tell her about turn on when you turn her around and spit presidents into her mouth, her auctioned pussy and against burnt cork breasts. Call her black skunk. Switch her smell from woman to machine from Harlem, history of home   to dumpster or dump her or dump on her. Call her brownie without sugar or portion control. Call her rhino. Ugliest animal of Africa. An impale. A scratch away of. Look apologetic then laugh away the sincerity. Call her honey. Crust yellow. Peel back the ink blots bubbling beneath her and leave enough stains to remember where to return to.

II. "   Hit the earth,
                    said looseleaf
                    elephant tusk
                    white woman.

                        Utilize mathematics to determine percentage of
                                platinum lineage

Grate pavement between hands,
gather room for an entrance

            {   *You can do this*
                                                                    }

        Chalk outline of learned behaviors   :

            Cross at ankles
            Elbows against ribcage
            Tongue against teeth   closed mouth   silence

when white man enters white room wearing white wallet and importance   show him
your onion skin

   pearl against licorice
   ear lobes
     enamel smile between
     midnight lips

      choose lightest shade of thunderstorm or
       flaunt darkest shade of snowfall.

                  "

Eiko, female, and Koma, male, rest hungry veins over soil and feathers and straw and crawl. Walls of scorched canvas with smell of sea salt and tamari ink grow around them, behind audience. They are sweet rice paste skin and skeleton of sixty year aged fetuses. Her yellow hand is slow motion toward yellow man who twice came inside her enough to build two babies, one at a time. As she twists, her bones crumble like campfire-seared paper. A nest of countries clasp their spines, dirt traveled across borders with invisible passports. Until mud of purchased weather wet their noiseless skin, they feast on electrically produced drink.

she rarely took the bridge or news from an unknown mother

Out of the pail, a foot. The problem is, there is no more room for mistakes like girls. Those toes were delicate enough to tag with repeated numbers of birth and death. The only humans who count are boys. In China, one-child policy pressed forth in '79, forces women to give birth to runaways. Between baby girl's legs burns a reminder from when mother held oil lamp to wrinkled skin to decide retaining value. Go fetch a bowl, big enough for baby, big enough for the warm water constructed for drowning. Call it Killing Trouble. Or, a troubled killing.

Would sex happen more if there were no letter combinations like AIDS or STD or HPV? Why can't forgiveness occur when mothers leave daughters behind? What is the shape of embarrassment found from the dismissal of love? If you can still smell her does this mean you are too close? Why are you so afraid of this body? Can one receive an allergy from a lover like pregnancy? Is it Sunday? Can you tell by the way that I walk? If I forget your name, will you stop existing? When does death become more than romantic plagiarism? Don't let me address you like a human? What happens when you put gender on a grid? How does place influence your work? How much of this is you? Do you stand, sipping on Brooklyn and weather veins? If I tell you, will you still find me beautiful? How can anyone begin anywhere when everywhere is difficult to emerge from? Does it make sense that she wants to be cut open with knives purchased from the bodega in the shape of torn apart razors just to remove her father's fingerprints? And she gathered? And she lied? How do bruises fail our bodies? Are you a man who has had sex with a man anytime from 1977 to the present? Have you had sex for money or drugs anytime from 1977 to the present? What is your distraction? If you work until you collapse, who will pick you up and soothe you back toward consciousness? How do you take away the carbon without maintaining the echoes of imprints? Why do you keep looking at the door? Do you call yourself a homo to get back at us for leaving you? Why do you wake in the morning? What is the sound stars make the moment they are seen? Am I queer enough? Would you notice if I amputated my life away? If I practice harder at being a boy will you fuck me like one? Why do they always thank *god* after winning awards instead of their bodies? Why didn't you take off your bra when we slept together? Will you watch me walk away? If writing is a prayer, how can I call myself an atheist? What is at stake? Have you ever taken Jesus into your mouth? Would you swallow? Would you go back?

part two:
on blood
and the tantrums of memory

she was sitting across from me on scratched vinyl and between us were hard candies. I chose watermelon because it reminded me of summer and picnics and spitting seeds from one grass patch to another. she asked questions as I sucked solid block of sugar from artificial fruit and pretended seeds were there in the center and challenged my fear of digestion. let's talk about your sexual history, she began. resistant watermelon chunk held onto back molar and hid. my teeth locked together and my tongue, still pierced by a hole purchased for forty dollars fourteen years prior from man in tattoo shop who stuck needle and stud and caused me to swell for over three days, worked hard to remove candy from possible cavity. have you ever had unprotected sex, she asked. and I grew relieved as candy fell onto trampoline of taste buds and I swallowed even though it was slightly too big and I'd probably receive a stomach ache like one receives a mischievous pimple or, in this case, a sexually transmitted disease. and she repeated her question and I thought about what counts as protected. one time when I was nine, I poured baby powder—the unscented kind—onto my vagina as though it were a ghost and let her rub herself into it. and my memory is a cube with muddled corners so I cannot remember whose fingers went where and if they even left our skinny sides, but she may have gone inside and were they clean and hadn't we just eaten cherry fruit roll-ups, so our hands were sticky. and can preservatives and corn syrup conjure up a disease. I tell her that sex never feels protected because if someone is inside me then a part of me is breaking and bodies don't come with doorbells or welcome mats or hand wipes and faucets. she assumes I am a straight line of vanilla fucking, with back against bed frame and dick plunging me toward matrimony or motherhood or at least a well-deserved orgasm and if I'm not demanding condoms then how am I not pregnant and do I think I'm immune to AIDS and other life-ruining letters. and this is when I reach for another candy because then my mouth will be too full to correct her or congratulate her for making me feel wrong. I tell her condoms don't fit over cunts and no one ever explained the intricacy of a female internal version to me, size more appropriate for elephant trunks or fists and maybe she could show me and why are they more expensive and harder to find? I crawl my list of sexual partners into her ear and mathematics become important when I find I have a three digit whole number with a remainder of three and does it count if it was shitty and does it count if it was forced and does it count if no one came and does it count if I was paid for it and does it count if I can't remember. suddenly she opens her mouth like a lion with the width of a pummelo and says, well, it is good that you are here now and begins to gather the materials to guide me toward a diagnosis. she lifts my forearm which is perforated like a notebook or war victim and cleans my skin with small white cotton ball. I want to tell her I need more cotton. I want to tell her I want anti-septic potion on every limb and between my folds and inside my pussy and all inside my parts that smell and seep and weep for me. but she cannot hear my guilt, so she cleans just one small patch of me before preparing my blood for needle puncture, before she prepares my blood for analysis, before she prepares my blood to know what letters I am

memory 831.

called me   AIDS faggot

I can tell by the way you wear sick

jumped sweater off skin
cracked neck with the sound of voice
knife-tongue
sword-swallowing fist
a rope
gun
strangle
removal of sneakers
gutted genitals and

wallet

are you a junkie
bathhouse bottom feeder?
on knees, you wear calluses and blow jobs
are you a homo
child seducer

are you bloody
dirty pores dirty fingertips dirty gums dirty skin
do not kiss me hug me sit on my toilet or
sit beside me on train or
at dinner table or
touch my kids or my money or use any of my utensils

do not give it to me

grabbed cup full of blood and
forced it out the window

     suicidal spree of cells

they fell against a window screen, slightly
popped out if its grip

fell against woman wearing hat and
impatience
thought it came from a bird or
spaceship

stirred into puddle from daily intake of
rain and spit

and remained

fences are meant for hanging
punishment for perversions
your blood is what remains of your sick
your spice rub of improper masculine
and bible dismissal

we sharpen our knives on you
pay attention to the disfigurement
of hate

what is queer
is   inborn
      from mother

you think: father rape

from nature not nurture
lack of breast feeding
or forced vegetarianism

what is disease
is contagious
from billboards or
                    brother

you think you can get *it*
can be rubbed off on you

          if you sit too close, all you will catch is
enlightenment

this diagnosis makes me want to jump up and down, smear what sweat on my body gathers onto a page and workshop the shapes that emerge. tell me I say cunt too much.   cuntcuntcuntcuntcuntcuntcuntcuntcuntcuntcuntcuntcuntcuntcuntcunt tell me I am aesthetically unpleasing due to inconsistent thread count, hair length, bulge against zipper that couldn't possibly come from an enflamed vagina but must be something purchased or surgically altered enhanced chosen from a catalogue or sent through the mail. tell me I am really talking about my childhood or responding to drop in socio-economic class or impatience of political warfare and white men and bullet holes piercing artificial limbs and women digesting pills to push sperm away from eggs because men forget to cover their dicks in latex and spermicide, allergic or repulsed by sexual/mythical desensitization. tell me to wear a band-aid because my blood is rusty because my blood is a callus of friction and was purchased in the east village for forty dollars and was used as a performative exclamation to show the imprint of red over white and drip over smooth and the show was sold out because blood play is really *in* right now. tell me what blood type I am because if I am oh negative and virgin with proof of unchartered cuntcuntcunt then I can give it away to anyone and you will give me money. if I claim this as my job occupation career path employment status will I receive a full benefit package inclusive of (mental) health, dental, prescription care, acupuncture, unlimited museum gym sex club memberships, twice a year pap smears on the house and complimentary admission to all exclusive clubs and organizations.   what do I get for giving you my cells. your family. have you been left behind in such a way that you can no longer go back. far enough that phone cords no longer reach. or static internet connection too bubbled with bad connection confuses the posture of your requests. I think about sewing a notebook to my back, like a suitcase to be written on and filled up as I move and tell no one of my destination. family starts out one way and warps with age and shifting. makes me think of mother who looks like my dna. standing next to her (sometimes), like wearing a pair of pants made for a child. zipper bites skin and fat bloats over fabric enough to cause breaths to bleed.   if breaths bled then we'd all be wearing surgical masks.   *silence is a backward motion*   I scream to be fucked but when you stick it inside me I fear contamination, spoilage, stain of the diseases you weren't sure of. at least fifty percent of sexually occupied americans will receive hpv in their lifetime. I am too old for the vaccine and it chose me several years ago. I suck on your erect blood and blow you toward orgasm. I drink a jack and blood, blood on the beach, tequila blood sunrise, pint of blood from tap. intimacy called art called bodies. run your blinks over every scar that line me like looseleaf paper ripped away from its glued casing. tell me what looks wrong or what feels right or what right/wrong body even means and I will airbrush it me away. i don't wait till i am

broken to make new roots[ξ] when I pull hard enough on these hairs, I gather the ellipses of blood, omissions of plasma and use as lubricant to pleasure myself toward death.

[ξ] j/j hastain

rubbed lip sore against bed sore and that is how you get it

should have squatted higher above the toilet so the germs waiting to be retrieved would not have jumped from porcelain skin onto me and this is how you get it

but he reached out his hand and expected me to shake it, slap my skin against his, and that is how you get it

there are times that hugs can work like ritalin or aspirin or chamomile tea or heroin or a soothing astringent to the entire body and this is how you get it

she placed her bubblegum in my mouth as I was yawning and I almost lost track of her cells when I placed teeth against each other and squeezed out the fruit punch bendable flavor and that is how you get it

the 2 train was running late, but it finally arrived as I was taking my last sip of slightly too weak coffee made from french press and I had run out of cream so it was bitter and I got on and left enough space between the woman wearing braids across and to the left and group of youths somewhere off to the side and then someone sneezed and I could not tell who and I do not believe it was covered by cupped palm and this is how you get it

in Vermont, we went camping and groups of men and women scattered around the soil in sleeping bags and tents and hammocks attached to tall trees and I woke up with bite marks from mosquitoes tired from a late night binge off blood savoring each one of us and this is how you get it

part three:
between legs a fist rises

Kyle licked my cheek in nursery school and called himself my boyfriend.

David Fiorina unzipped his first grade, seven-year-old dick from inside cartoon covered briefs and revealed the difference between boys and girls. This was the beginning of cock envy for me. I thought: if I pull on myself enough, it will grow long and flimsy like his.

Mrs Schwartz. With afro of perfectly placed grammar. Kaleidoscope of commas and semi-colons.

The boy who lived on my cul-de-sac named Jamie or Gregory or something multi-syllabic who tried to grab the slab of chest where my breasts were meant to be and I bit his wrist.

Allison's baby powdered vagina placed against my bathed one and the way they felt mashed together.

Shannon Dole. Platinum hair on head and perfectly matching everywhere else.

Denny, who fell against pavement, and died before I could ask him if he'd be my boyfriend.

Gene DiNocci stole his mother's honeymoon bracelet and gave it to me on Valentine's Day. I returned it on St. Patrick's Day.

Anthony Barnado raped a girl seven years after I gave him my phone number.

Red-haired Jennifer Kine who had the same birthday as mine and shared first tattoo experience upon turning eighteen. While her boyfriend paid, I fingered her with my left hand and pulled on her strawberry roots with my other.

Jennifer Polari with an accent from the Bronx and a small mustache I never needed her to hide.

Jennifer Dilley broke my cherry in Freehold, New Jersey in her parent's backyard beneath plastic swing set where mosquitoes gang-raped my body.

Dustin was too young but I fucked his mouth with my clit anyway.

Michelle had calves like a curved building, hard and approachable.

Andrew became an ice-skater and moved to Delaware.

Erica recognized me in the mental hospital but ignored me at school.
That time after group therapy when I put my tongue in her mouth and she bit it.
And said: *I just wanted to steal one of your taste buds.*

Diane in blue Cadillac, whose brother became my roommate and drug partner at nineteen.

Rachel, the thin one.
Then, Rachel, the fat one who became skinnier than the thin one and no longer seemed as appealing.

Chris grabbed my ass with her Jamaican accent, then took a shower before allowing me to fist her.

Kathleen fingered me on the floor of her best friend's boyfriend's apartment after we snorted coke off our palms.

Renita had a thing for vampires and sushi and I almost slept over due to her impressive thread count.

Tom paid me to fuck him. Then, Tom paid me to fuck Debbie, Kina, Sasha, another Jennifer, Helen, Rita, Barbara, and the others.

Deanne opened the door, wearing an Irish accent, offered me warm orange juice, told me to take my pants off.

Leonardo was never a good kisser, but he smelled like linen and ocean.

Gabriel from Chickopee tried to fuck the gay out of me and almost
got away with it.

take what you want, what you need...and all the rest you can leave behind

They come to New York with these dreams with these poems with these visas with these blue jeans with these poorly typed resumes with these record deals with these childhoods. They forget about winter coats and cannot afford electrical outlets. A couple of ways to pay rent include exchange of blood for needle and cookie and good deed. Or place cup beneath penis like top hat to shrunken head and squeeze out particles of reproduction. Or place pillow over head while strange man exerts orgasm beneath above against you and make sure to collect cash upon threshold access. Or pass out splinters displayed on rectangular shards of paper on street corner several blocks from university where one day you will be a student. Or stick longest arm into rusted cans where garbage grows like scratched off tumors and gather up plastic glass bottles toward their promised refund. Be careful of bed bugs, wet spots on subways, men who follow too closely behind, credit card APR rates, identity fraud, and gay cancer. Take what you need, what you want and leave behind your rest.

She forgets to wash the apple before placing between teeth before rinsing her mouth with fruit carcass before red waxy skin splits open her expensively pushed together molars and remains until flossing. She is not told by professionals with teaching degrees the importance of placing condom over penis before placing into mouth before taking tongue over newly gorged veins before gathering the right questions to find out the risk involved with orally charged correspondence. She calls herself a virgin because she has never taken her pants off because you cannot make babies from placing erections into mouth because AIDS does not happen to white girls in high school who give head behind the gymnasium. She misses class the day they discuss HPV the day her teacher quietly mentions oral sex as a gateway to vaginal penetration the day she would have learned the risk of receiving this human papilloma virus by placing boy's harden particle down throat and swallowing.

The disruption of pagination against a well-lit screen.

Man handles glass of beer like a woman whose waist is made of blown glass.
A book assembled from electricity and computer scientists and formulas
and a memory board made of metal purchased overseas.

Woman interrupts man's inactive page-turning by asking him about his bookshelf.

I fall in love alphabetically, she says.
Turn-ons include separated genres
with carefully placed labels stuck to edge of unfinished wood.

He pushes fingers over screen of book with disemboweled splinters and binding and
remains an anorexic version of technology.

A swirl of fingerprints can make the letters grow taller, though nothing can compare to
the smell of paper glued into signatures pressed into clasped vertebrae and shelved
between its peers.

Workshop a poem on paper or body. Masturbate on belly or back. Begin with accessories such as circles through ears or red war paint on chapped lips. Locate hair upon chin or beneath arms on experimental woman and when you kiss, press the shards of fur against her and twist. Inscribe a book with someone else's name. Whisper: *what disrupts you?* Then, disrupt her. Flip hand over and use lines from curled palm shell to draw a building. Bring enough copies of your sexual history for everyone to learn how to properly eat out a woman. Practice the angular motions of disintegration.

There is too much to do but I think about nooses. There are poems forced out like morning push from twelve-pack night. Do not give me that disease yet because I still need to find my way back to her and I have yet to experience India outside of New York restaurants and I don't even know how to speak German or Arabic and I would like to accomplish a full head stand during yoga practice. I understand the scars. I can fathom punishment and perishing. There is too much to admit so I think I will watch television. I will go outside and push the girl out of me into someone who likes that sort of directness. I can tell you something. I can kiss you like your mouth is an empty journal and my tongue is the poetry that turns pages into magic. I can show you something. I can tell you that five years ago I fell onto concrete and lost my chapstick and got nine stitches without proper plastic reconstruction. I can cry at commercials and walk across bridges without jumping. Please just give me eight more months of this year before you give it to me. There are still books to be stolen and trees to climb. I understand the circumference of Brooklyn but how long before you stop distributing medication from insatiable pharmaceutical monsters and just remedy this fright.

A cigarette after the third glass of red wine, which misleads the color of lips and fills in the gaps between teeth and porous tongue and spreads her open enough to kiss her and call her amazing and use adjectives that can also describe a traffic accident or hip hop song and when their bellies curl toward each other they forget to breathe in and they forget to compare sizes and they pretend not to notice the awkward exchange of hands in hair or on hips or grabbing half of her ass because grabbing all seems too forward and when morning arrives, they are half nude and half sick and repentant so there is guessing about what to call this what to call her how to approach one another after groins have been explored and the indulgence of disorder and nicotine and bodies have worn away.

Water is saltier on the west coast, but a passport must be ordered before crossing into Canadian territory. How necessary is love when death is closer and never expects a phone call in the morning. All photographs have been removed. Please scrape her out of the brain before breaths can be executed. Drunk is when she feels most like curving into available potholes and falling asleep. Stacked books in every corner symbolizes a healthy reader, or someone trying to hide. There are enough rooftops outside my window, so I forego drapery. At night, nudity pinches skin and the mirror held against wall by six nails absorbs her reflection.

Is it enough to be called beautiful.
A piano drips lashes of rhythm onto paint-stained window.
They refused to fondle her poem when it hid beneath her sweater.
She brought a pomegranate to class, split it open and called it her womb.
When she digested the seeds, they could not differentiate her blood from the fruit.
It is cold enough to freeze her hair into hardened drips of split ends.
Rush out before the morning turns into Monday.
I'd rather be called intricate or genderless.
They could not remove the patches of her cells disgracing the expensive,
immovable instrument.
When everyone was checking their voicemails, she was peeling away the language off her
skin, threading the words together and knotting her way toward a hanging.

I hate this self without your climb.

Color admitted to be less enthused when you left that tear on my face. Your pull of ring through nose deepened my energy for your slope. I am waiting for your moment to collide in me again. That fiddle-head fern burrito with quinoa and cactus and my fear of heights almost second-guessed your kiss of cilantro against my crooked bottom teeth and when the moon arrived, it was ours for the evening like jukebox quarter pick. That photo of furred plant rising between your thick, Czech fingers. Yellowstone hot springs oozed what stirred within me while you took Eastern European Canadian lap and let me learn it. Remember: the socio-economics of pubic hair and fisting. Remember: when you cut my knee with your belt buckle and turned another scar into me. Later, the bullet hole from our canoe trip when I fell into our wooden couch named log while cooking lunch called macaroni and final array of vegetables. You turned nurse while I cried away my fear of body dissection. Soothed away my fascia, held my limp, my worry and made love to me while pup climbed carcasses far from view and sky turned into crayon box of seventy shades of blue and breath was everywhere. Warmed oats over body to soothe the mosquito bites, to quiet the rage of sting from nettle, to laugh away the texture of skin's sleep.   I am dying.   Mother got into another car accident and sister thinks I am drugging. Father wants me to wrap my lost inside passport purchased only for *your* border and get out of this country that haunts me.   And I cut myself.   And that time that we went to the theatre and both got triggered from women's beauty secrets and tragedies. I climbed into bed beside bathroom and kitchen and living room called studio called nook and you climbed into your sari-draped sleep cave and we carved away what needed an exit. Years later, another woman wants to know why I'm fleece and not silk. Sticks fingers inside me and calls it sex. Remember the bathroom. The cabin. When you gave me more of your gender and I explained my preference for multiple-choice. She does not like to be penetrated and is afraid of coming. So, I go. And on Friday, I am passed around a room full of costumed pansexuals. A man with stubbled cheeks kisses his curiosity into me. He calls me beautiful and I spit my slime toward the back of his throat. When I grab his wife, I think of your eucalyptus laugh. When I pull her into me, I smell your storm, your knots, your calluses. Before I am permitted entry, I must remove my coat because I am wearing sneakers, though heels are preferred but far more uncomfortable. The notes on my windshield and in my black converse that waited for me outside of classroom at Buddhist university. Pink post-its with your ink curled in. Will you search for me.   I fondle the dreadlocks you rubbed into my red and the few that arrived on their own. Before I fall asleep at night, I scream my loneliness toward the west and hope that your pacific will push it into the salt and sea you call your view and remember who I am.

This leather is not simple.
This springtime rain curving into my sneaker's gaps makes these flat feet curdle from moisture.
See the world before it slips on a banana peel and breaks its back.
Paralyzed poems may disrupt breakfast or evening digestion.
Do not inhale the scent of her or you will forget your limits.

> I will never forget how you take your coffee.

Today, your head aches.
Tomorrow, your thighs will rub themselves into tiny bumps like jellybeans.
You took the moon away and now buildings run into themselves from lack of light in the evening hours.
A picture of your feet crossed ankles with hair like soil smudge.
I ruined the lean in.
Cigarettes have begun to fornicate with my lungs again.

> I forgot how you take your coffee.

So, they are miniaturizing giraffes as pets and some man in Long Island feels the need to strangle away prostitution. What is this but a night where photographs of birds fly into windows and patchouli elixir works as vitamin E on art project saturated forearm. Are you ready for this?

She gives birth to four orgasms that night. He only paid for two. Three-quarters staged like the play she saw the previous evening. There are shivers of removed skin beneath her. This bed is graveyard and her body is corpse preparing. This man is virus and his breath is weaponry armed. The woods. That beach. The chipped paint and rust infused dumpster. A scattering of body parts like confetti after New Year's. His confession sounds like a favor. It's not like anyone is missing them, he says. It's not like they are human anymore. Somewhere in Washington or New Jersey or Oregon or Wyoming, a mother still sets the table with one extra in case she comes home. Then, the phone rings.

the blue in your hippocampus matches the blond in your amygdala

If there is no photograph, memory will blur the entire moment away. She never loved you. That beach with that glass and those rocks with rings of Saturn smell of salt never existed. There was no dog. Cupboards of curry. Oil-drenched latkes after tashlich and the sunburn over breasts like latex cherry sweater without buttons or itchy tag. Poison ivy. Lust. Cigarettes when drinks tasted better with tobacco and a tongue licked dry. Roasted garlic. The time I sat in driver's seat with tense knees, learning standard stick shifting three pedals from you. Your cunt after proper orgasm. Sunday morning. New York Times sold in Boulder on our fingertips. Terra cotta cleavage in the tune of Beirut. Despair.

Wait beneath the doormat for update on
war correspondence and serial killer body count.
Silence rings doorbell of housewife without husband.
Fingernails are meant to be bothered by teeth not metal clippers.

Cause of death:

    deodorant application and razor burn.

A good day is when no one touches me. When fingers do not curl like cockles around neck. Friend is a word like noun, complex disturbance of rules and regulations. Lose me. Thrown into metal, into potholes, onto curbsides, over desks. Help is a word that goes ignored. An engagement of power. Eyes were once blue and now black has arrived. Lonely walks home from school after the push and stone throws. Lunch launches itself into me like soggy body. Peanut butter on shoulder keeps me fed until supper. Must I hang from a tree for you to notice.

Don't have to be described as repentant. Drink all night because you are thirsty for a blur. Four walls allow removal of brown paper bags from bottles shaped as obelisks. We have no bridges here, so death is far from reach. Happy hour is found all day from bedroom to cafeteria. The unfortunates are on the other side, where windows come with metal rods and doors lock three ways.

Blame low body temperature and knights of armor skin frame
for wrinkling mucus membranes and nerves of flesh on humans.

Armadillo.

Tails like severed snakes stuffed into their backsides breed lumps toward deformities.

Nocturnal digger.

Omniverous mammal of leprosy spread native to southwest United States.
Plates of bones across body like trash heap after Thanksgiving.

Stealer of smooth.
Evolution of bacteria.
Disease of virulence.

When tomatoes are picked too soon, disappointment is plunged into mouth from seeds too crunchy. Red skin like calluses from playing too much handball. She was not going to call, instead gathered her days onto sheets of cardstock and newspaper clippings. Awake, to the sound of horny cats climbing unshaved claws into fence posts. Why are you not verbal with me; does it make you uncomfortable? Her lips looked so happy in that photograph, as though she had just been kissed. I have been blocked. You must look up. You must. It looks like a full-figured woman sleeping in the sky. Am I the only one to notice the night?

You're so pretty, you know that, right? Follow the gyration of travel from Brooklyn to Queens or Amtrak to Toronto. There will be gunplay replacing the blood play because they could only get approval for bullets. Show me your feet. In an empty field where dandelions nap over clovers and music plays from speakers shaped as clouds, a girl loses her underwear. The wind travels north today. Want the sun to run into your chest cavity and burn you into hospital gown. Poles are meant to humiliate bodies. Show me how you bend. In a year from now, you may see sadness blown up onto canvases hung on walls and you can sit inside my nightmares. You're the prettiest one. What's beneath that? Wonder about your childhood and if all white men enjoy twirling for half-nude women wearing matching bra and panties. How flat is your belly? He will sit beside you and stuff store-bought whipped cream cake with chocolate sponge layers into mouth and forget he is diabetic. When he sings you happy birthday, he will omit most of the lines.

Outside, a cigarette is placed between lips of former addict. And then a song plays and eyes attempt a parade of tears until the loss of moisture becomes realized. Doesn't it just move right through you? A night grows thick and love looks best on scratch paper. Moon, if only I were not so afraid of heights; I would climb up there and push neon strip between thighs. This is unsafe. When I die, will you play at my funeral?

A phantom of all dreams is responsible for water weight. If you speak dirty to me will I need to shower more often. Here is what will happen: a yawn, a discourse of sexual appetite, childhood carvings from shoulder blade and razor blade, training belly to digest an entire apple including seeds and you know they are poisonous, will cut hair, will gather one to four more tattoos, will travel to another continent to get over you, will return back to brooklyn and find you waiting wearing gloss of photographs, more poems, return of habit such as smoking, late-night food binges, cocaine or pill thievery, awkward self-pity. You will speak your language to someone else and I will assemble another disease that cannot be pronounced. A surprise like tulip twisted out of homemade garden on a late night walk back to crown heights. As organs get known by new people, you will fade from memories. I'll be left, trying to get it right.

Until I hear my name called, I will wait with paper ticket in palm and ankles crossed like bowties and book against lap to cover the stains and you behind me breathing yellow daffodils against my neck and the shifting of your polyester skin comforting your bones and the dimple that only grows on your cheek when you look at me. To save a tree whose leaves have shed green toward brown, we steal roots and speed highways to be free from sirens and earth's restrictions. By fire. By gun. By mother's ignorance. By bathtub. By belt unglued from loops of pants. By pills. By heart suffocation. Gather this music as though it is morning as though it is ocean as though it is saliva as though it is the remains of me. What might have been lost has been stolen by someone else. Gone by midnight, teeth crumble inside melancholy mouth and questions collide into silence.

The spread of a notebook lets the light in. Butter replaces cream in coffee and arteries become greased up machines sliding out of bodies. We can get hotel room. You will stay with me. By the water, yellow black-tipped banana skin sleeps over cigarette remains. The ash. The corpses of rolled labor. Luggage replaces company. Amsterdam water replaces New York City buildings. What is a nomad, he pronounces. When I walk, I search for language, but do not want to commit to sound or schedules. Dirt clings to the crescent moons called fingernails. Call it Brooklyn's refusal to be left behind. Fingers are its passport. Body becomes camera documenting this search.

Pigeons cry out in wails. No Brooklyn accent, just long vowel sounds here. Who is waiting to be left: the one with hammered skin digging self into ocean   the one with grease-blood and tight pants   the one who does not blink   the one who kissed me on railroad tracks and lifted my shirt high enough to locate spherical distractions   the one with tattoo on ribcage and spit of ink   the *one*.   Man with lips I'd like to detach and place on my pillow for when I need a kiss afterward, asks me about soul mates. I tell him there cannot be such a thing, since our soul is never sure of what it wants. Distance can remove the stain of longing, until jet lag pushes tourist into pavement and bruises are served with breakfast. Eileen reminds me to think about poetry. She handles my waist and fondles my earwax. The smell of tobacco here is romantic like Brooklyn Bridge reflected against NY skyline at 9:14pm. You should have lost your fingers inside me at that moment. I would have let you but you prefer beds and door locks. There is an allowance of one cigarette pack. Each inhale is hungry and reminiscent of early morning digestion of rainy filter and chemicals. Sip of see-through city satiates me until supper where I spread unmelted cheddar cheese on whole wheat bread and eat in two parts. Graveyard of bottles in canal mixes with loose petals and it is almost beautiful. Are you too high to play rummy 500 with me?

I have hid this part of me since it began. Suffering can be found between toes that curl from the institutionalized madness of high-heeled oppression. There is no past of what we were. Prayers can be substituted for food if necessary and man with Greek skin alerts me on the logistics of torment. Do you see this. All these red dots. Call them abrasions from too much air haunting skin away. Dutch man does not leave his home for fear of contamination by oxygen found outside his windows and doors. He is called crazy and given pills to swallow in the shape of peas with his peas. No one waits to see if he is right.

You are authentic like curry or weathermen. Sirens become six-piece band accompaniment to acoustic musician and I am outside your window waiting for you to notice. There is a scar that connects your eyes like a drawbridge and it is about to be kissed. A pause of coffee from hot to bearable enters mouth the way you used to. A tree belly dancing with its leaves wants you to name it and when you do it weeps joyful tears of maple syrup. See me live life in public on computer screen. Remember when you fell from the bed and hit your head against the sink. You cried with your entire face and body became a raisin curled into anguish. That was the day you announced your number. That was the day we spoke about adoption and love. If I scar and you do not see it, is it real? If I fuck and there is no pleasure, does it count? For you, I keep my legs together until they part and I pretend the entire time. Sounds can be heard from shared wall but I promise you they are empty and without purpose. On Tuesdays, bees cry when flowers turn inward like turtles, closed and napping. When the stick of honey is gone, one must turn toward the bitter.

Yoko Ono squints her handwriting on white spackled walls at Museum of Modern Art. She tells me i am beautiful. When your name drips out of my sheets, i cry. Did you know blue brings out the best orgasms. Heels lift to kiss the curve in your upper lip. There is a taste of mint. The water is troubled and i notice reflection of your hand against my shoulder like lee used to do with camera angle and shutter speed. How about you compare your moving on with mine. You climb sugar-soaked mountain while i climb salt-soaked humans. Did we not touch enough or was bed too large to remember the importance of back-bending night holds. Bike ride to bodega to purchase broom large enough to sweep you out of the soil. Memories are not chosen and break-ups never end. The worst that can happen is i blurt out love into pierced ear of shortened woman.

Are you blue?

Boy with night-stained eye travels back and forth to fence purging sickness, homelessness, aluminum glass canned bottles sucked on for warmth.

Man compares one knee to the other to woman wearing afghan of exhaustion, introduces himself as cancered and hypochondriac'ed.

Hearts hurt when lovers lunch on lawyer diagnoses rather than each other.

Do you cry with green fingernails painted on holiday and torn stockings with your mother's skin rash beneath the thread pattern?

She is quite sure she will die today on a bike in the rain with a cloud shaped like an orange above her body and a pothole to catch her belongings and a dog to smell her fall and a bus and a blue jay with bald patch on its right side and a baby sleeping inside pushed carriage and a traffic accident where no one is hurt but a taillight and a stoop sale sign missing its date and time tacked to nearby light post and a screaming man on fifth avenue and a garbage overflowing onto curb angering tourists and a hotdog truck pushed into the shade and a father who will die upon finding out her true identity once they spill her open.

Have you read the number one best seller?

On a Tuesday, woman wearing seven learned languages approaches poet wearing red-haired scars.

God is detangled from Sodom and Gomorrah and boy dies but arrives back on earth to write book about heaven in mother's handwriting.

I see your stains, the arrest of your sins.

They will imprison you for lying, spitting, cussing and pre-marital fornication. Homosexuals are just people who have been seduced by early fingers.

Who seduced you, she asked.

Your scars are what keep you from the memory.

Green, plastic table supports the lean in of accusations and if God is just a word so is homo and hell and love and forgiveness.

There is too much prayer and not enough living.
They are bringing people back, she announces.
I can tell where they came from because they are scared.

I want to know what your fingers feel like inside of me.

There is a man who stretches his dirt over ripped back like birthday present packaging.
He is Ukranian homeless holding onto wife wearing pants past knees to prove she is his.
Exposes the intimacy of gums when she smiles.

Boris, I wonder why you left the red in.
Was it laziness or hedonistic expression.

After museum, she feeds me saltless-rimmed glass and cigarettes.
Tells me my mouth tastes like orgasm.
Unhinges her jaw to investigate further.

At night, we remove our zippers, while laps become balance beams for clitoris and head bobs.

Hands erase unwanted genitals and charcoal new ones to replace the gap.

sunset.earthquake.loneliness.

Now you have touched the woman.

Crying in public is only prohibited when love is involved.

It was a sunset that caused eyes to swell like staph-infected foot and she remained until bloodied red orb fell down from height to bridge.

Shake head from body.

Try not to talk for too long because they stop listening after the third sentence or first poem.

Stop staring at her mouth; it is there to confuse you or eat away at your refusal.

Does it bother you that you have no friends or are friends just a bother?

We deal with over-population through starvation. Use empty paper cup as wallet for tourists to fill on hot day in June when guilt of privilege is at its height. Press metal over rubber beneath sneakers and tap for change on 3 train toward Brooklyn. Walk onto benches wearing bed bugs and carve middle name into third panel because you forgot how to spell the first one. There is red static projected over brick and if you watch, notice the dogs curved over breathless body. The dandelions are delicious, though something in that wish wears away my lifeline. As I cross the street, notice the man slicing death into his neck.

You smile beneath corduroy cap, the one lost during a bike ride in June. Send a message. It is more like west coast rain, not strong enough for umbrellas balanced over hairstyles. Sometime after 4 pm, I went into narrow pharmacy where woman with limited hearing and stalled color against scalp sold me a dark blue umbrella for $5.43. Scolded cash register for not explaining the amount of change to give back to me and I wonder how long your hair has gotten. Ten toes evenly placed on two feet brought me into bar, which I took you to once and we kissed because we did that then. Everyone curved fingers around plastic beer bottles and I held up the wall with my lean. Am I too old for this. Out the door to the right and several blocks down purchased me a pack of cigarettes. I could barely wait to burn three layers of my throat with tar meant for driveways or potholes. I notice the color of yolk staining the bottoms of my fingers.   Should I panic.   You have one hour left in your day and I am one hour into a new one. This rain sounds like pennies thrown against emptied cans of vegetables or a stampede of tap dancers whispering their feet over puddles. I miss you in a way that cannot be helped. A lather of one thousand showers to ease me toward a new lover is not enough to excite my orgasm into existence. There is too much loneliness on a Saturday when rainbows clasp wrists and I wore the red shirt we made together celebrating home.

There is an exquisite corpse among us.
The smell is reminiscent of Connecticut bar room and nervously inhaled cocaine snorted off belt buckle and navels like uneven dance floors.
Analyze the flirt from grammatical errors and misinterpreted use of adverbs.
Your zipper, like my tongue, does not want to remain in place.
Leather wraps bullet-holed measurements against swallow.
Yellow tie around wrists and we never discussed a safe word.
Tattoo of broken blood vessels from the pull apart of stubborn thighs.
I have never heard of that shade of blue and yet you compare my right arm to it.
You stole the underwear back that I took from you and replaced it with white cotton shirt, which smells nothing like mechanics, but more like hyacinths or bodega-grown lilies.

A shoulder covered in constellations that remark in the daytime. Hands look best when weaved like grandmother's quilt. If I promise I don't have anything like contagion or pre-set alarm clock, will you let me stay? How long did you wait once I left before you scrubbed me off your skin. In the summertime, scars need no black-light detection to form stares. She blames it on unnecessary childhood and rough sex or razorblades that grew dull on forearms and wrists. Music can tell you I'm in more than like with you, but teeth turn into traffic accidents when articulation is tried. How dirty am I. Lady at the park tells me I'm ruined. We are this way because of traveling fingers and repressed hard drives. Miles Davis will blow me into another poem and loneliness will accompany me out the door.

Sleep with paintings to smell the intent of imagery. Photographs cannot help but flash against the back sores of homelessness or helplessness and the gap left from her walkaway. Throw up your tired and filthy, said grey. Gather all the dirt left from others and sculpt a new front door with window and embroidered welcome mat. Grey fingers squeeze it open. Grey thighs, like three-day old newspaper, blurry and smudged. Grey kiss grows grey tongue into grey receptacle for cavities and chewing. Grey history cannot be understood without insurance-required therapies and pharmaceutically-produced medicines. Testify a protest to see body's grey response. Grey lonely lasts until just past five a.m. when finally her knots fall asleep and she wakes up a sort of breaths.

You ask for cold beverage without ice and use straw as pen to carve out the wax behind ear.

What that stare means is there's no time for good timing.

Yellow cake tastes more like deflated eggs dead from sugar and whipping.

Squeeze tears from eyes like improperly placed pimple and pretend the excretions don't celebrate you.

What is love but a series of cancelled television programs.

How to explain the burden of this armpit hair and sore throat from inhaled intense and the reminder of rain against soft rooftop like your manicured fingers over hard clit.

Tell me.
There are seven different ways to look at
paralysis
exposed nipples
electric violins
and your childhood.

Don't leave just because the sky weeps and you have no umbrella.

You will miss this.

He might suggest to qualify the why. If poems are breaths, and to stop would require death, there should be less funerals. Red wood purchased for two dollars bullies the words away. Meditate it toward something new like fourth of July firework slide show or Picasso warping. Does that change things? End with vulnerability and remember to remove your clothes slowly. What remains continues like compost thrown into front yard garden. Those squash were not planned but when peeled and eaten taste almost like her. The earth plays hide-n-go-seek beneath ocean. Disgruntled knife slices moon shape into fingernail and the hot cherry peppers taste traveled, a commuter sauce sliding over pasta, digested with red wine. How long did it take to type them out of you. The letters formed from their tongues and homosexual resistance. No one can know I let him grab my breast and suck the soap away. Can I say no even before the question is asked. No?

Distract me away from these last two cigarettes. Stay away from what bangs against sewed-in zipper. Never assume there is such a thing as one *or* the other. In choice, comes indecision, then the desire for both. Hiccups grow inside body like convulsing peacock feathers tickling pattern of breath. Ties wear men on subway in morning choke of pre-formed workday. In the eve of night, necks disrobe. How often do you shave the genetics from top upper lip and if I handcuffed you to a bed, could I watch you grow? Women wear smooth because they are handed razors and panty hose at birth. Do you miss the color of your flesh before you paid them to color you in? I am worth leaving because once this is over all that will remain will be my hair on your pillowcase.

Grow arm long enough to measure diameter of moon and prove its perfect half. It is smoky tonight. There is fifty-five percent cocoa in this pink wrapped poem, with savory raspberries and solid dark chocolate and why my waist wears grey cotton skirt at night to allow room for breath. You notice me. There is a father mentioned. The discontent with store-bought pizza dough. Parade of rats play tag on street moments before your mouth mounts mine. A hand is sleeping over in your traveled scent and you don't mind this in-between? Gender slurs into pierced ear. When lace gathers against hipbone and crawls into slit of ass, it means nothing more than drag for an evening. Pretend I am a car that cuts you off on Flatbush Avenue. Touch me with rage of middle finger fury; I like that. Choke my words out, which seem to require paper and black ink. Bruises can be used as paint-by-number guide for later. I cannot speak this. Instead I grab my parts as though these curved fingers are yours, redden my clitoris until it bleeds a new shape like thimble or severed hook, and backpack across this body.

One.
Silver fish climbs over kneecap already dressed in dusk and distractions. Lonely sock crushes its vertebrae and the slivers of texture assigned to its torso. There is no guilt in this.

Two.
Jar of peanut butter with spoon licked almost clean drips three serving sizes into panicked mouth. When it is too late for supper, call it midnight breakfast.

Three.
Consume addictions like sexual partners without the condoms or orgasmic interruptions. Replace yoghurt with nicotine and listen for the gurgle of blood gather in charred lungs.

Four.
Three calories are burned when toilet seat is pushed back into natural state.

Five.
Pull hair with fingers. Spread cells out like breadcrumbs to prohibit the getting of lost. Tumbleweeds of fur will speak your travels far better than postcards or online postings.

Six.
She arrives just past midnight with chocolate and cologne painted neck. Her jaw is a museum of kissing. They climb into night clenching poems. Practice mathematics while watching rats march through street wearing curious gazes.

Seven.
Packed paint and a brush thick enough to close up your pores. Packed lace because it represents the gender I am not. Packed Bukowski, Burroughs, Whitman, an extra fold of underwear, something sexy, something borrowed, something broken.

Eight.
Is there a difference between climbing away and climbing toward? There was a contemplated jump on rooftop with drunk sun sliding toward a stupor and single cigarette in mouth and a phone without cord and three women in the background talking about university or dish washing techniques and I just didn't want someone to have to clean up my bladder exploded upon impact.

Nine.
The remains of minus eight months left in this body and nothing like a baby ever grew inside me. Will I miss this?

Ten.
Great hair. Can I take my picture with you? Touch her tits and you will save the world, one squeeze at a time. Will you play with me? You have blood in your hair. I'll pull it out so you can make a wish.

lose track of alcohol consumption and ego or
what is love but a singular syllable of panic

Written with Thomas Fucaloro

You are the one who dangles gender on knitted rope of floss, pre-washed by teeth, hang history up to dry like black-and-white photographs in dark room dressed in red light. No, no, no, no, no. But *you.* You close your eyes when you steam open lungs, pre-washed by herbs grown on fire escapes, medically attainable with photo id. You flutter those lids like blue jays or pigeons convulsing on chicken wings. Are you alphabetizing your brain stem, which do not bleed like your best friend, but have been fried from too many pills and not enough meditation? You gather up words like I hoard condoms and orgasms. You speak about booze as often as I masturbate. Tell me about Adrienne Rich and Charles Bukowski. Compare this summer day to an automobile, overheating on a highway built in the ocean collapsed by a mountain tagged by graffiti artists. Got three shells of varying sizes on desk, size small, painted red like burnt atrophy. They arrived from the Atlantic on a Monday when children gathered sand and cigarette butts in bathing suits and I emptied rage and silly heartbreak into saltwater spill. Learn how to swim by attempting to drown. Swallow enough sodium to raise blood pressure. Oh. *You.* You offer to increase population by handing out babies, snort family and poetry rather than weather forecast of addict remorse. I am hungry.   Devoured your obituary with knife and fork, serrated and inaccurate. Perhaps your forehead hit the wooden plank of barstool or pipe curve, while pockets grew into tourniquets choking you away. No, no, no, no, no. Blame the combat of blood bruised into bodies. Call it war. Lose passport and formalities, huddle into something like a backyard with exposed tabs and smoke arriving from cavities.   Knees gather palms like fleshed napkins and   and   panic consumes dissected language swallowed hard before the arrival of sobriety.

Notice how the poet's long unsobering moves with grace of a harpsichord but growls with fanged venom bite, a lady bug. Oh you are such a cute little poet lady bug

consuming the beats of everyone's heart into a wing   a flutter   a move along with the rain

the blood can't hurt ya.

You'll notice today's poems are brought to you by the letter i and this poet here does a wonderful job of giving you energy and red and strength and red and empowerment and red and tender and red and gutterific rupture of the intake valve that can't handle the out take of human existence. You'll notice how this poet's voice pitches high-low-high-low-peaks and valleys, light to dark, exhaustion to that first kiss of the thigh hummmmmmmmm and you'll notice now how the poet will seeminglessly blossom some rage and venom into matters of the heart fingered……let's observe

There is an emotional disturbance of map tinctures as nipples explode into sky like presidential promises. What is this but a night where photographs of birds fly into windows and patchouli elixir works as vitamin E on art project saturated forearm.

Your genitals disrupt the alignment assigned to me through Kinsey's finely-tuned scale!

Mouth attached to my face sketches a kiss onto yours.

[**Are you ready for this?**

Charcoal dip your fingertips.

They are miniaturizing giraffes as pets and some man in Long Island feels the need to strangle away prostitution.

You want to tell me what you mean by this reliance of bathroom stalls for insight?

Enough numbers and poems and pluses and threats exist on linoleum tile adjacent to the flush for mathematics to be perfected   and suddenly higher education and overpriced universities cannot compete with barroom water closets.

Whatever disease *my* borough has may be attributed to the bridge connected to yours.

Notice how the poet starts right with the nipples. Nipples are a huge part of poetry and the more sensitive the poem gets the more erect they get. The poet chooses this path because it's that monumental moment where tongue and mouth meet breast, a nipple almost down the throat. That's why men have Adam's apples, They have nipples of poeticness down their throats.

146

Also in poetry nipples tend to represent facisim but I think this poet isn't a facist, just someone who likes nipples and how they rainbow.

You'll also notice how the poet's voice is like a perfect swan dawn that warms ya up just enough to let you know you're alive.

It's good when poet's remind you you're alive. They are that one beat that measures pulse and this poet's pulse is a full on onslaught of life.

Let's watch how this poet slaughters death by singing life and life sings a tune called.....

(sing)

Leave. Unmarked.   Bo-o-o-o-o-o-o-ones.   By the side of the house.

Get your fingerprints all confused by recycled New York.

Boys and girls expire early due to sociopathic side effects and the allure of camera angles.

Love is vulgar enough to replace bathing   food binges   habits like hair removal and skull punches.

Grill.   Marks.   On.   Rib.   Cage.

"dear mom when I was eleven I tipped my toes into your bedroom and found a kitchen appliance in the drawer beside your bed where you also kept your pills and gardening sheers when you trimmed your hairs at night and practiced surgery beneath your nightgown and when I plugged it in—the appliance not the scissors or pressed medicine—I heard the whirrr that I read about in Judy Blume novels. dear god, it's me and I'm debilitating arteries, vague antecedents confusing pronouns. it likes to be touched she likes it pitted they grab onto each other and rip it.   what does it mean to yearn only half way   "

CONDEMN!

linoleum.
question marks.
knee pads and ankle weights.
motherhood.
male contraception.
New Jersey.
fireworks.
your hand on her breast.
prostitution.
feminism.
four-wheel drive.
personalized license plates.
fostercare.
lactose intolerance.
heterosexuality.
looseleaf paper.
republicans.
uncivilized healthcare.
gun permits.
border restrictions.
immigration laws.
mountain top removal.

war.
animal limbs.
buckets of guns.
taco bell.
aids.
burnt eyelashes.
dental floss.
heart palpitations.
tumors.
happy meals.
happy feet.
happy tumors.
happy nostril flair.

happy testicles.
happy lord Byron.
happy hangnail.
happy homosexuality.
happy in the sense sunrises.

And that's all you can hope for not just from a poet

but from the people around you

a sense

of sunrise.

Dying so softly each day yet our poems are flourishing.

When you snap a pencil in half

you still have a pencil in one hand

and something to shank someone's ribs with in the other

and that's how you write a poem

lead in one fist

blood in the other.

The grey lady told a story about a boy walking home from camp on a Tuesday wearing backpack and paint beneath fingernails. In Brooklyn, he walks on cracks that remind him of his mother's spider veins which she hides beneath stockings and blames on poor circulation and forced employment at local shopping mall. Dollar bill crumbled into corner of front pocket is all that remains after splurge of candy several minutes earlier purchased from nearby bodega. He reaches old age at eight when local man lures him into truck, and decides to tear him apart like Super Bowl Sunday hot wings. Police in blue and anger knock on door after several days searching. A confession bleeds out with ease. There is a finger, erect, on man's left hand and it points to his freezer. Boy's foot is behind the ice tray. Head is with perfectly lined shoes in hall closet. Hide-n-go seek haunting of limbs. Boy's pants hang on chair in kitchen. The dollar still remains with one forgotten piece of candy he never got to.

The tip of two noses pressed like grilled cheese into sandwich and a cold is brewing in the summertime. How many minutes per day do you think about death. How long before your jump is gathered into the air toward pile of cigarette corpses not thick enough to cushion spinal cord. Mondays are meant to deliberate, masturbate, hurl suicide notes against pillowcase, dyed red from wet hair traveling into cotton fibers. What does it matter that she loved you once or that you won that award or that they clapped after your last poem or that you got that degree or that you survived childhood and that late night walk when that man tried to slice your face open or that you asked her to marry you and she said yes but now it is just a __________.

To save a life, learn how to build furniture. Use hands to measure the distance from wooden foot of chair to back rest. Remember when you taught me how to play guitar? Learned the span of time between each finger, prohibiting the spread. You called me hazel. Followed by American. Ended with *I love you.* Match-making may be dangerous when mother arrives on second date. Compare coffee table to love affairs: hard, awkwardly-shaped, pointless. I want your moon to look like mine. Did you notice my looting of your red lacquered flecks of nail paint? Your Turkish fingers forced all the color away and now it is mine. All the existence to be seen has happened. Life is the past tense of poem. Love is the present tense of death.

Author Photo by Jay Franco

Aimee Herman, a queer performance poet, has been featured at various New York venues such as the Happy Ending Lounge, Dixon Place, Wow Café Theatre, Perch Café, One & One Bar, Bowery Poetry Club, Public Assembly, and Sidewalk Café. She has performed at reading/performance series such as: In the Flesh erotic salon, Hyper Gender, Sideshow: Queer Literary Carnival, Mike Geffner Presents: The Inspired Word, and Red Umbrella Diaries. Her poetry can be found in *Clean Sheets*, *Cliterature Journal*, *InStereo Press*, *Sound Zine*, *Pregnant Moon Review*, *and/or journal*, *Polari Journal*, Mad Rush, Lavender Review, and *Sous Le Pavre*. She can also be read in *you say. say.* and *hell strung and crooked* (Uphook Press), *Focus on the Fabulous: Colorado LGBT* Voices (Johnson Books), Best *Women's Erotica 2010* (Cleis Press), *Best Lesbian Love Stories 2010* (Alyson Books), *Nice Girls, Naughty Sex* (Seal), *Women in Lust* (Cleis) and *The Harder She Comes: Butch Femme Erotica* (Cleis Press). She currently works as an erotica editor for Oysters & Chocolate and curates/hosts monthly NYC erotica and GLBT lit readings. She can be found writing poems on her body in Brooklyn. Find her at: www.aimeeherman.wordpress.com

Made in the USA
Monee, IL
07 July 2026

56551611R00092